Here's Mike

Here's Mike

&

JUNKYARD GRANNY, WHISTLING BERNIE SMITH, THE ROBERTSON SCREWDRIVER, PANCAKES & ETERNAL TRUTH

MIKE McCARDELL

HARBOUR PUBLISHING

Harbour Publishing Co. Ltd.
P.O. Box 219, Madeira Park, BC, V0N 2H0
www.harbourpublishing.com

Cover photograph by Nick Didlick
Edited by Ian Whitelaw
Cover design by Anna Comfort
Text design by Mary White
Printed and bound in Canada

Canada Council   Conseil des Arts
for the Arts   du Canada

BRITISH COLUMBIA
ARTS COUNCIL
An agency of the Province of British Columbia

Harbour Publishing acknowledges financial support from the
Government of Canada through the Canada Book Fund and the
Canada Council for the Arts, and from the Province of British
Columbia through the BC Arts Council and the Book Publishing
Tax Credit.

Sales of this book help support Variety—The Children's Charity.

variety
the children's charity
Global
BC

Library and Archives Canada Cataloguing in Publication

McCardell, Mike, 1944–
    Here's Mike / Mike McCardell.

ISBN 978-1-55017-562-2

    1. Vancouver (B.C.)—Anecdotes. 2. McCardell, Mike, 1944–. I.
Title.

FC3847.36.M47 2011   971.1'33   C2011-904624-5

This book is dedicated to Judy. I've never met her. I was buying a bottle of sparkling wine for my daughter's birthday and the nice woman at the cash register in the liquor store asked when I was going to write another book. I said never. I was through with book writing. I didn't believe anyone read them.

She said her mother had read all of them. She said her mother had breast cancer and read them while she was going through the turmoil of pain and despair that goes with cancer. This woman at the cash register, Angie (I knew that from her name tag), said her mother told her she found comfort and relief in my books.

I was shocked, and humbled, and didn't know what to say. My books, my writing about ordinary folks usually overcoming daily problems, gave me a reason to live, but I didn't think they did the same for anyone else. I paid for the wine and got my change. What's your mother's name, I asked.

Judy, she said.

Then I stopped before leaving the cash register. This didn't make the person behind me very happy. I was holding up the liquor line. Okay, I said to Angie, I'll write a book and put your mother's name in it. What else could I do? Her mother wanted another book.

Angie started crying.

Another clerk saw her and asked her what the problem was, meaning, "Is this guy bothering you? We'll call security and have him thrown out."

"Nothing, no problem," Angie said. "They are tears of happiness."

What choice did I have? Judy wanted another book. So I started, and since I can't just stick her name in a story, there is only one way to do it.

This book is dedicated to Judy.
You are a survivor. I learn a lot from survivors.
Thanks, and good luck.
Judy, this is for you.
Mike

Contents

1	This Is Not Electronic	9
2	I Like to Write about Simple Things, So: Worms and Scooters	12
3	What Is Ahead in These Pages?	21
4	Things You Don't See on a Tourist Map: Junkyard Granny	23
5	Sunday, March 20, 2011	32
6	A Super New Unbelievable Recipe: Pancakes	37
7	Chasing a Bus	41
8	Okay, Let's Get Down to the Absurd	44
9	Money in the Mud	53
10	Another Strange Route to a Good Destination	57
11	My Wife Told Me to Straighten Up	66
12	A New Home for Ruby	69
13	The Love Train	74
14	A Little Education	82
15	Whistling Bernie	88
16	I've Got a Problem	92
17	High Points of My Life	96
18	Cardboard Ocean	100
19	Germany Taught Me Everything	108
20	The Day the President Was Killed	114
21	Inside the Prison	120
22	Stop the Presses	127
23	Carmela and Luppo	135
24	Pike Place Fish	142
25	That High-Flying Leaf	147
26	This Incredible City	150
27	The Family Album	154
28	And the Name?	159

29	The Big Trench Story Again, with a Better Ending	162
30	The Good, the Ugly and the Amazing of History	167
31	Bitter Tasting Sugar	173
32	The Chicken Shack	177
33	Island of the Dead	180
34	The Net Minders	184
35	Bagpipes, Coincidentally	190
36	Hockey Town	196
37	The Biggest Game	201
38	Hockey Before It Was Soured	207
39	The Artist and the Ball	211
40	Rita and Ida	214
41	Rolling Down the Hill	216
42	What Happened to the Chicks?	219
43	Flowers in Her Bike Helmet	222
44	The Singing Grocer	227
45	The Stanley Cup of Lawn Bowling	231
46	Street Hockey	236
47	The Doll Collector	244
48	Les Paul	250
49	Stolen Bike	254
50	Can't Have Things, So Have Things	260
51	The Ice Cream Cone	263
52	The Vacation Home	268
53	Fence Post Hole	273
54	Laughing Hand	277
55	Eagles in the Sky	286
56	Teddy Bear	290
57	Last Chapter and Your Assignment	294

This Is Not Electronic

This is a book. It doesn't have a battery. You can drop it and it won't break.

Books are good, even if they are old-fashioned. You must reach up with your right hand to turn the page. You can't pretend to turn the page by touching a tiny computer and then watch the page pretend to turn. You must actually touch the paper. This will burn up about one calorie every five pages. Reading this entire book will reduce you by a quarter pound in page turning alone. You don't pay extra for that.

Books were invented long ago by those who wanted a place to hide their money between the pages. That is why people go to used book stores. They hope to find a hidden $20 bill.

Some people will look at you like you are strange because you are reading a book with hard covers on the outside and pages inside.

They will take out their hand-sized plastic thing with a see-through front and say, "I have 5,000 books in here."

You can say that when you are finished reading this you will have one book in here and point to your head. One book in your head beats 5,000 in your pocket.

You can also put your head down on the book if you get sleepy. It won't be comfortable, but it has been passed by the Canadian Health Board as not being harmful. If you lay your head on your little plastic thing it will hurt, and you'll have tiny electrons bouncing off your brain.

In times past when boys fell in love they carried girls' books for them while they walked home from school. Boys and girls no longer walk home from school. Their parents drive them. And girls' parents will not allow anyone to borrow anything electronic from their daughters. That rule applies especially to boys who are known to be after girls' electronic secrets.

Books are also good in bookcases. They make you look like you know many things. You could look up those things on Google, probably on a hand-sized plastic thing, but that isn't as convincing as having a bookcase, with books. "Did you read all those?" someone will ask. If you nod your head, no matter what the truth is, you will look like you know many things, even without Google. This is very impressive.

One last thing: By reading this book, an actual book with ink, which comes from ink wells, which are like oil wells only more rare, you will be participating in one of the greatest intellectual revolutions ever in the history of all histories. When the first books came out people said, "Nothing will ever be the same. We don't have to wait for the monks to make copies of the royal gossip anymore. We can learn everything from books. We can also lay them on the floor and stand on them and reach the highest shelf in the kitchen where the chocolates are hidden. Nothing can stop us now."

Small hand-held plastic things will probably take over some day. But with this book you can say you have something from the past, something you can leave in the bathroom and someone else can use it without a password. And, most importantly, if you lose it you won't have to kill yourself.

Also, if you are caught in a deadly shootout on the street, this book, properly positioned over your heart, might just save your life. Until then, it just feels good in your hands.

I Like to Write about Simple Things, So: Worms and Scooters

If only we had gotten that, a picture of it. The work day would have been over in ten minutes.

The family—mother, father, two kids, boy and girl, so perfect—all looking down at the sidewalk in the rain.

What are they looking at?

My gosh, or OMG in current text talk, it hit me and the cameraman at the same moment. Wonder, delight, we knew what they saw and it was a gift from the story god.

A worm. They had seen a worm on the sidewalk. A poor, lost, confused, blind, helpless, naked worm, all alone, lost in the wilderness of concrete. Pity overwhelmed me.

How quickly can we stop and get the camera out and run across the street and talk to them about this discovery of nature?

We stopped with a jerk. This was a fireman's stop. You don't slow down. You stop and move at the same time, which in truth means for me sticking one leg out of the mini-SUV and groaning because my wife made me go to the gym again last night and I ache.

The cameraman is already in the back getting his camera.

Making up for my legs, my heart was beating faster. Actually I love worms. When I was very young there was a crazy man on our street who taught me to appreciate worms. He would wander the black asphalt of the street and the concrete of the sidewalk after a rainstorm looking for lost worms and rescue them. We didn't have gardens or grass, but we had cracks in the sidewalk and places where weeds grew and somehow worms were born in those subterranean socio-economically deprived conditions. It was kind of the ghetto world for worms, no lush lawns or composted soil, just cracks and some decaying pigeon poop to chew on. These were tough worms.

But when it rained the ground got saturated and, just like in the suburbs, the dirt filled with water and the worms had to dig their way to the surface or drown in their tiny dark hovels. The rich, upper-class worms that were born in the suburbs had grass to wiggle through while waiting for their basements to dry out. The city worms were stuck on the sidewalk.

You know a worm can't see. There is no need for eyes when you spend most of your life underground, but during those terrible times when you have to go to the other world, up there, on the surface, eyes would be a bonus. "Where the heck am I?" a worm asks. "There is a large, flat, rough stone below me and I can't seem to find the end of it. Plus I feel wind, which I have never felt before, and I hear horns and footsteps and they are very close and I am scared."

How could you not help feeling a kinship with a lost worm? They're not the ones that poured concrete over virtually every inch of their world. They weren't asked if poor living conditions would by okay with them. Like many who live in poor neighbourhoods, no one thought about them. All they want is a sliver of dirt to disappear into. That isn't asking much.

The crazy man in my old neighbourhood would pick up lost worms and return them to the patches of weeds. He should have been made into a saint, except everyone made fun of him. One day a nasty, mean young punk in the bar on the corner of my street stepped on a worm in front of him and the crazy man hit the punk and killed him. It was a rough street.

Actually the crazy man didn't kill the young punk. The steel edge of the stairway that went up to the elevated trains did the job when the young punk's head hit it. That was seen by me as divine intervention, but that didn't help in the defence.

The crazy man went to jail for a long time, but after that I picked up a worm one day and brought it home and put it in a jar filled with dirt and kept it as a pet. That is, until my mother found out what was in the jar. I don't know what happened to the jar. It wasn't there the next day.

But I have loved worms ever since, and when the family was looking down at one on this morning after a night of rain in Vancouver I knew we had a touching story. I knew how to write it because I had spent a lifetime thinking about it and anything less than a lifetime put into a story, any story, is cheating.

The camera was almost on the photographer's shoulder when we saw the mother use her shoe and kick the worm off the sidewalk onto some grass next to it. Owww. Ohhh. Then she kicked it again because the first time was only a glancing blow. Owwww, again. I was yelling in my head for the worm, which has no voice. Can you imagine being naked and cold and getting kicked, then kicked again over a rough, unnatural sidewalk, even if was meant to be an act of kindness? Poor worm. And then the family walked on.

Darn, I said.

We spent the next two hours driving around the city without seeing another single slightly off-centre sight. We drove, we looked, we talked, we drank coffee, we talked, we looked, we looked for a bathroom because we have drunk coffee, and then someone in the front seat says, "I can't do this anymore."

Someone else says, "All the young reporters in the station think you have it so easy. All you do is work twenty minutes a day and watch someone picking up a worm."

Then someone else says, "We will find something. We will."

I know we will, because every day, as I have said in every book and every speech and to everyone who asks, yes, every day we start with nothing and come up with something. It is the same with life. You can start with nothing and come up with something, if you keep looking and trying and believe you will.

That is the philosophy that has kept me going for more years than a television anchor can hope to hold onto stardom. The others have to keep smiling and be pleasant and be informed and be congenial and witty.

I just have to keep looking.

The method of operation is this: You keep trying, you keep hoping, you keep believing and it will happen. I guarantee double your money back if it doesn't. That is the business plan of every successful inventor, tycoon, religious leader, politician, community activist, lover, parent and general good person since the Neanderthals started taking up with the cute *Homo sapiens*. It works.

And, yes, they did. I read about that in *National Geographic*, so we are all actually descendants of interracial couples.

An hour crawled by. It passes quickly when you are having fun. Our time dragged. We drove until we saw the couple who were washing Greyhound buses. That would be perfect. We got out. They didn't mind being on television, except they had just finished their last bus for the day.

They offered to wash it again, but we have integrity. We never stage anything or have people do things for the camera. I once got upset, as upset as I ever get, when I watched a young cameraman move a tag on a tiny, just-planted tree so he could get a better picture.

Never, never, never. And I said it again. Never move anything. If someone sees you doing that, what will they think? I'll tell you what. They will think we set up everything to look just the way we want it. They will think we stage events and outcomes. They will tell their friends that you can't trust what you see on TV be-cause they move everything around to suit themselves. So, never, ever. And therefore, no, we cannot watch you rewash that bus, even though it would mean we would be done and happy and could stop driving in circles.

We left and started driving in circles. We passed a house on East 6th Avenue where I met a man a few months ago in his front yard cutting wood to burn in his stove. This was a block from Clark Drive. Don't get lost in your thoughts if you have no idea where that is. The point is the man told us that when the house was built it was beachfront property. Now it has streets and a park and more streets and cars and railroad yards and warehouses and factories and then more streets in front of it. (You can read about this later in a special chapter of its own.)

Meanwhile he had a photo of his house when False Creek was more than twice the size it is now and the house was near the edge of the water. In the picture a woman is rowing across where now six lanes of cars drive on Great Northern Way. But I had already done that story.

I stopped to say hello to the man. "Anything new?"

"Nothing," he said.

The biggest physical change in the history of the city had

taken place in front of his front yard, but as for something new? Nope. Not a thing.

And on we drove. Somewhere there is something. Remember, I believe it.

Yes, but where?

Left. Then right. Then left again. WAIT. The little girl is on a scooter and her father is helping her balance. STOP. This time I am out before the truck actually stops, which is a dumb thing to do. Even with the wheels barely turning, the reality is unavoidable. Your foot hits the stationary ground. The SUV is moving. You are in between. Whoooo. I am staggering to hold on to a door that is swinging open and I'm trying not to fall on the ground. I am sixty-seven years old and supposedly a mature person and I'm stepping out of a moving vehicle in front of a little girl on a scooter with her father about to protect her. And yes, my legs are still aching, but I don't care.

"Hello, I am from Global TV and is this your first day on your scooter?"

Right about then, if I was the father, I would be stepping between my little precious one and this stumbling mad man. Luckily, I was not the father.

"Yes," he said, he being more composed than I.

"And is this your first day on your scooter?"

"No," said little precious one with a large, wisely placed helmet on her head.

Okay, I thought to myself, because you have to think very quickly when things appear to be going badly. My life has either just hit a new low—I will never get a story despite professionally believing I will, because, let's face the obvious, this is not her first day and I can't do a story saying, "Here's a girl on a scooter, which is nothing new to her"—or the day will be saved because there must be SOMETHING here that is new.

Let me interrupt again. "New" is so all important because New things are what make News. If you get a bunch of new things together, like the king was caught not wearing any clothes and the enemy's armies are advancing and too much vitamin D is bad for you, those things become NEWS. That is the plural of New. More than one New. That is really all there is to it if you want go to into journalism, which is a fancy word that means writing in a journal, which we no longer do since Facebook was invented. All you have to do is find new things and write them on a piece of paper, which we no longer have but if we did you would then have a NewsPaper, which you would shorten to Paper, as in "What does the paper say about vitamin D today?"

"Vitamin D is now bad for you. That's news."

Of course, newspapers are now read on your little hand-held plastic device so they are no longer called papers.

What is in your hand is called the media, like all television and radio and computers, which is a term invented by a Canadian a long time ago meaning anything that has a message. That Canadian was Marshall McLuhan, a brilliant teacher from Winnipeg who said things so brilliantly not many could figure out what he was saying. He became rich and famous doing that.

His most famous saying was "The Medium Is The Message." That became the explanation for everything in the '60s. What he said to explain what he was saying was that radio and television were an extension of ourselves, so whatever we were doing was there for us to see and hear what we were doing and therefore we were broadcasting ourselves to ourselves. Imagine selling a million copies of a book for saying what was obvious. The guys and girls who drew pictures inside caves of themselves hunting deer knew they were broadcasting themselves to themselves. But they weren't smart enough to come up with a catchy one-liner to say it.

Anyway, the point of all this is that news has to be new and a girl riding her scooter for the second day is not new.

Then I saw she and her father were standing at the top of a slight incline in the sidewalk.

"Is this the first time you are going down that hill?" I asked. She nodded.

Oh, my heavens—OMG again—we have a story!

She went down the hill with her father holding both hand-grips of the handlebar and his precious little one screaming and I could have kissed her helmet or her scooter or even the worm that, through a route full of circles, led us to her. The story was wonderful. It was touching. It was delightful.

Why?

Because a little girl screamed and shouted, "Hold on, hold on, Daddy. Don't let go." And all the while he was not letting go. Of course he was holding on. He would have died before taking away his hands, but the picture of him running along with the scooter and her screaming was universal. He was helping his daughter grow up and protecting her at the same time.

If we hadn't paused for the man with the old house and the bus washers and the worm we wouldn't have found the girl. Had we gotten there one minute earlier the father and daughter would still have been on their way to the hill of screams. We probably wouldn't have seen them. Had we arrived a minute later it would have been over and they would have been at the bottom and we would never have known about the courage of riding down the hill for the first time. So much of life is made up of flukes.

Obviously the moral is don't give up. Good things, new things, can be waiting just around the corner. You are thinking bad things could be waiting, too. Nope. That won't happen if you don't want them. You always get what you want, if you really want it.

After that family earlier in the day had kicked the worm onto the grass, we waited until they were gone and we checked the worm. It was heading back to the sidewalk. You can't quit helping just because someone makes the same mistake more than once. We picked it up and carried it to the dirt around a bush far from the concrete.

That took only a minute. We found the girl and the scooter in the one minute window that was open to us.

What Is Ahead in These Pages?

It is probably obvious that I like three things. At least it is obvious to me.

That is, three things after the important things in life: my wife, my kids, my grandkids, my friends and breakfast.

I love simple stories on the street. If you have been watching me on television you already know that. For more than thirty-five years I have worked in a television newsroom and largely managed to avoid real news. I have looked for worms instead of car crashes. Worms and kids and flowers and shoes in the middle of the street give me meaning in life. This is not profound, but it is fun. You could do it too.

Also, I love Vancouver. You probably know this because I have done hundreds of stories about what happened in the past on a street, any street, when there was mud and no litter. Vancouver is so young and it grew up so tough and bare boned it is impossible not to want to be its friend.

You know I came from a big city, New York, which I also love, but New York is so big you never get to really be its friend.

It is always your mother or your father, or both at once. It tells you what to do and stays pretty much in control of you no matter how old you are or how long you live there. Other giant cities are the same.

In Vancouver you become a buddy, a girlfriend or boyfriend, and you grow up together.

And I love my own life, which in some ways was like this city's. The kids on my street in New York had no money. That's not a complaint. No one had money. We didn't have swimming pools or even know how to get a subway to get to the beach. We swam in piles of cardboard boxes two stories high alongside a factory. Cardboard gives you better memories than chlorine.

I love the life I have had, which is made up of growing up in New York and coming to Vancouver and finding the stories that have shaped my life in both places. The closest I can come to philosophy is this: Wherever you are is good, or you can make it that way. Who you are with is wonderful, or you can make it that way, too.

I know that is impossible. Unless you believe it.

If I were able to, I would divide this book into three parts to make the reading easy for you. Then you would just have to pick out what you want to read. But I can't. When I do a story on East Hastings I think of the Skid Road that was once there with oxen pulling out logs so big it was close to impossible to move them. The past overlaps today. Then I think of Times Square in New York, which was a thousand times worse than Main and Hastings when we came to Vancouver. It was my training ground in crime reporting. It is now as clean and safe as Disneyland, and so I know the same can happen in Vancouver.

All the stories fit together. So that is how they must be.

Things You Don't See on a Tourist Map: Junkyard Granny

Speaking of worms and flukes and timing, and believing good things always happen eventually, this is weird. You know you are not going to get ordinary stuff in here, but this will stretch your credibility. I still don't believe it.

I had an early morning coffee with an old friend, John McCarron. He is the cameraman whose daughter was killed in a car crash more than a decade ago. We spent a lot of time together after that, growing quite close. He is now fighting cancer. We talked and had a few laughs.

When I left him I picked up my wife, who was taking a bus to work. She never asks for a ride but I try to help her as much as possible because I am usually on the road. Plus she usually has an amazing story about what last happened on the buses. She takes the East Hastings bus. I try to keep the stories to a minimum.

Anyway, going to her delayed me by a few minutes from meeting the cameraman who was assigned to work with me that day, Darrell Patton. Actually, it did more than delay me. He had

23

time to clean out his truck and organize all his equipment and take a nap.

On my way to meet him, a bus driver I know called to tell me that the old fire engine in Stanley Park was on the back of a tow truck. That's the fire engine in the playground near Second Beach, and once a year it gets hauled away for painting and to have the tires pumped up. I don't like taking suggestions over the phone, because by the time we get there to whatever it is it is usually over.

I met Darrell and apologized for being late. Then I told him that someone had told me the old fire engine in Stanley Park was being towed away for repairs.

He told me that would be fine, but reminded me that last time we worked together he had suggested we try the unexplored world over the Pattullo Bridge. Surrey: the land of comedy. He also pointed out that I have done a thousand stories in Stanley Park and only about six in Surrey. His number on the park was too high, but he won me over.

When I first toured Canada in the early 1970s there were Surrey jokes even in New Brunswick.

"What's Surrey?" I asked.

"You don't want to go there."

I went. It is fascinating. It is the fastest growing city in Canada. It is a trailer park turned into a metropolis. It is farmland that has become thriving communities. It is home to so many wonderful people, but it has a reputation based on half a dozen streets that is hard to shake.

And those streets are right over the Pattullo Bridge.

If this were a tour book it would say, "Welcome to Surrey, but if you drive over the Pattullo Bridge you may die." The bridge is too narrow for four lanes, which it has. It has no divider down the middle except for skinny plastic orange poles that were installed a few years ago. They would have put in orange cones, but there wasn't enough room for the cones, which are fatter than poles.

If you drive at night or in the rain, pray.

If you make it to the other side you will see they are getting rid of the pawnshops, the prostitution, the junkyards and the characters that go with them, some of whom have the appearance of being unsavoury.

For decades they were the welcoming committee for Surrey—hence the reputation.

However, Surrey has probably the best mayor in the country, or even the continent. Dianne Watts should be prime minister. She keeps making Surrey better, and I only know of her through the media. I don't live there and I can't vote for her, but she has done many amazing things, and the best thing she is doing is putting the new Surrey City Hall right in the middle of that old run-down neighbourhood.

Down will go the pawnshops. Away will go the bad people and up will come a polished civic centre with good people going to work and play.

You want a solution for any problem? Do what Dianne is doing: put something good in the middle of something bad. It takes courage, but it works, every time.

Back to crossing the bridge, and the worm.

Darrell the cameraman made a left turn just after the bridge and suddenly the world of Surrey went back to the world of tired old jokes and good people who are trying to change that.

We were in Bridgeview, completely isolated from the rest of Surrey by a highway, a river and junkyards.

There are only about 700 houses in Bridgeview and some of them have junk cars and scrap iron in their backyards. On the same street are houses with beautifully landscaped yards, flowers in front and back and on the sides. Flowers here, bumpers there.

There are still some open drainage ditches that make it difficult to get around after heavy rain.

Nonetheless, the residents fiercely defend their community. It has character, it has strength, and when you live with a junkyard next door and a highway down the street you either love it or leave.

We knocked on some front doors with junk cars in the front yards, but no answer. We went down a back lane that had junk cars on one side and junk cars on the other, and there, right in front of my eyes, a living, breathing person. Once you find someone, whoever they are, as I keep repeating, you are halfway to wherever you want to be.

What good is a marriage without another person? What good is friendship without one of those? The only time it is good to get away from others is when you want to be alone, and as soon as you are alone what do you think about? Another person. Or God. And that is only if you are a believer. And if you are a believer then you are thinking about what? Another person, although an extremely large and powerful one.

But for me the best thing about this person in the back lane was that she was a woman. I like women better than men because generally they are nicer. This one was pushing junk into a junk car.

There must be something about the junk that we can put on television. That means there must be something that will be interesting to half a million people. Junk? To half a million? But there MUST be something.

She told us her name was Dianna and she was trying to get as much scrap iron and metal in the car as she could before it went to the crushing yard. The heavier the car, the more she'd get for it. It was all legal and all based on the scale.

Okay, this is basic economics. Try to make whatever you have worth more. That is a good lesson, I thought, and that might be good enough to tell everyone tonight—until I realized everyone already knows this.

Hey, did you know that if you have something and you add something more to it you can increase the value of it and then you can sell it for more?

So? That is basic knowledge. If you have change in your pocket and then put more change in, you have more. This is supposed to tell me something? There must be more to this story that is not yet a story.

She said she drove a tow truck. Now you're talking. But in truth, women doing wonderfully creative things are common now. Women cutting open brains and fixing the insides. Women running corporations. Women driving tow trucks. Forgetaboutit. What woman doesn't?

What else? I am waiting. And hoping.

The company she works for is called Cheap Towing.

Now we have something. Comedy. Are you kidding?

No. She shows us the side of the truck. CHEAP TOWING. You can't beat truth in advertising, but how do you tell that story and make it longer than, "You know there is a company in Surrey called Cheap Towing?" Ha ha. "And they don't charge much."

"Yeah, so?"

"Cheap towing. Get it?"

"Yes. Please, move on to the next joke."

Lesson. Don't try to be a stand-up comic unless you have a million one-liners, all memorized and all good.

I didn't have a second line.

Anything else?

She first walked into Cheap Towing when she was seven. Her mother worked there, in the office, and brought Dianna along so

27

she could babysit and work at the same time. The baby loved the excitement of being around bumpers and broken lawn mowers and kept coming back. She eventually went to work there.

Interesting. I am struggling with this because I believe every parent should bring their kids to a junkyard at least once. They will never forget the rows of cars sitting in the mud with no wheels and their hoods open waiting for someone to rip out a part. It takes the romance out of cars.

Later, when they see the commercials for super-expensive cars on TV, cars that can make you feel like a man, or a woman, cars that can give you individual power, cars "that were made to drive" (like what car wasn't?), they will remember the open hoods. And they will say, yeah sure. Just give me something that gets me there.

But I still don't know how to turn the story of Dianna into the story of the night.

"There is nothing else about me except I am going to be a grandmother soon."

Bingo. Zoom. In fact, like the car commercial, ZOOM ZOOM ZOOM. Magic. Perfect! Thank you!!

"Who? When? Tell me!"

I am so excited I could burst. I don't know much about life, but I know that being a grandparent is the best thing about it. I have never won a lottery or had a million-selling book, but I am a grandfather and that has made me happier than anything else, ever.

She said her son and his girlfriend were expecting in a month and they knew it would be a boy and his name would be Jordan.

"I will take him to the park and hold him and, well, you know. It is just so good, I can't wait," she said.

I knew.

She hugged herself with iron-strong arms and calloused and

greasy hands. She hugged a baby boy who was not yet born. She would be the kind of grandmother kids brag about.

That was all she did and that was all she said. That was all she had to say. A universal moment of joy that is only known to those of us who are lucky enough to live long enough to experience what was about to happen.

That was the story. It did not need any buildup or elaboration. Dianna, a tow truck driver for a company named Cheap Towing, was going to be a grandmother. The greatest story, the beauty of life, was happening in front of me.

I stepped back to let Darrell take pictures of Dianna stuffing old chairs and a lawn mower into the back of a car. I was in heaven.

I looked down. There was a puddle in front of my shoes. There was a worm that was thrashing back and forth under the water. I am not making this up. I don't do that. It was in the last moments of life. It couldn't breathe. It was drowning.

It was a painful death. Worms have feelings. All things have feelings. When you can't breathe you don't have to be told how bad the next few moments will be. It had been swept into the puddle by the rain of the morning, and death was a gulp away.

I reached down and picked the worm out of the water. It struggled in my fingers. There was some good that came with the junkyard—Dianna in rapture and a worm taking breath. I walked across the lane to a spot that had grass growing beside a fence that was around some junk cars and dropped the worm there.

You have to make sure when you do that that there is enough space for the worm to get underground before wiggling back out onto the asphalt or the gravel-covered back lane. It would be so sad to save a worm only to have it crawl back into no worm's land. Imagine what the worm would be thinking, and they do think:

"Warm fingers, I can breathe, cool grass, I am so happy, whoops, hard stuff again, no way out, what did I do wrong?"

So I dropped the worm in a finger-sized gully and wished it luck.

The story was touching. No, it was beautiful. Any expectant grandparent will tell you that.

On our drive back to where I'd left my car parked, Darrell stopped at a gas station to get a candy bar. Yes, grownups are still kids.

I stayed in the company SUV, just me and my thoughts about how happy I was that Dianna turned out to be a grandparent in waiting. Darrell had parked on the side of the gas station and I was looking out at some cherry blossoms in a back lane. Under them was a parked truck with the motor running. That is stupid with gas at the price it is now. It must also have been a company vehicle.

I saw a hole in the clouds. If you have read any of my books you know what I believe. We will cut right to the chase. I thanked the hole in the clouds for letting me meet Dianna. I do that a lot. The hole in the clouds is how you get through to what is on the other side. Don't mock it. You never know.

And then I thought, did you in the hole in the clouds lead me to Dianna for my sake, or did you send a rescue mission to a worm?

If I hadn't been there at that moment, that one moment in all the history of the world, that one moment in Bridgeview, Surrey, the worm would have died. So? It's only a worm, which is a very small thing.

But remember Dr. Seuss's "Horton Hears A Who?" Go read it now. Put this down and read about Horton the elephant who hears a Who on a speck of dust. We are the Whos in Whoville. To a worm a worm is not so small at all.

I asked the hole in the clouds. Did you send me to Dianna because of the drowning worm?

I was looking out the windshield of the parked SUV and I was thinking it is a stupid thing to ask a hole in the clouds a question. You think you are going to get an answer? And if there was an answer do you think it would be, "Yes, you were sent there to save a worm."

Do you think that is insane? Of course you do.

But just as I asked the question—snap! Two branches loaded with blossoms from two cherry trees that had been hooked together broke apart, free of each other. Right in front of my eyes, like two fingers snapping, right then, they came apart and waved in the air. Before that they looked like one branch.

How much of a sign can you get? I don't believe in signs. I don't believe that any celestial power would make two branches unhook just at the moment I asked a question that needed an answer.

No one would believe that, not even me.

Of course the branches had been tangled by the wind and of course they came apart then at that moment, just at that moment, because of the wind. Of course that is not an answer to a question idiotically asked of a hole in the clouds.

But they did come apart, and they came apart with a flourish that I couldn't help but see, and they did this just at the moment I was wondering about a question that couldn't have an answer.

The answer was that the worm did get to live another day or two and Dianna did make many people feel good about approaching grandmotherhood and the only way those things could have happened was if we arrived there at that moment. And that only happened because of the delays along the way. But I also liked that the branches came apart, just then.

There will be no more worms in this book, promise.

But I still like the way things turn out.

5

Sunday, March 20, 2011

The horror in Japan is still overwhelming. It has gotten much coverage. It should get more, even if a friend of mine has asked me why the media has to show all those crying faces, over and over.

Because they are crying, I said.

He said we did it just for ratings.

I said again, they were there because they are crying. The ratings are because people care, and that is why we show it.

"You do it for the ratings."

This is where bitterness and seeing things differently have their Berlin Wall.

"We do it because it is there."

"Say what you want. I know why you do it."

We all have our ways of looking at things and blaming others when we don't like what we see.

It is reality. It is only a week and a half since the tidal wave, and the suffering and the pain have only gotten worse.

In the past we escaped it through newspapers. Reading that

the agony was overwhelming has little emotional affect. It only leads to the next sentence, "Pleas for help have gone out world-wide," which only leads to the turning of the page to look at the horoscope.

Yes, I am critical. Yes, I am angry at those who blame the media for showing the pain close up. We are the same people, no matter what country or colour or path to whatever god we follow. We hurt. And when someone says we shouldn't show that, I cannot talk to that someone.

Something else is bothering me. I have heard since the earthquake:

"Do you mean my new Sony flat screen 3-D will be delayed? But I want to watch it."

And another thing. Despite what my friend said, the news about Japan is already fading. Libya has taken over the main stories and, when it comes to Japan, just how many crying faces can you see before you want something new? At times it is not a nice world.

I don't own a monopoly on the pain. I believe pain should be shared, but just how much sharing can you take? Your little girl should be held in your arms when she breaks a cup. Your neighbour should be called when her husband dies (and you shouldn't say you can't call her because you don't know what to say). And your attention should be on the TV when a country is blindsided.

However, the scheduled extent of the coverage on Japan tonight on Global is one brief update on the nuclear reactors followed by ten seconds of a prayer service for Japan in Christ Church Cathedral downtown.

I think the human side should get more, but I have a series that is supposed to start today on the history of Vancouver. I was asked to do this weeks ago and I was only too happy to oblige. I love the old stories and I love Vancouver—and I won't have to hunt for stories this week.

I have spent weeks preparing.

This morning, Sunday morning, March 20, 2011, a new young cameraman and I were out shooting scenes around Vancouver and copying historic pictures from old books. It has taken longer than I hoped but we've made it before the deadline. I got to the TV station at 4 p.m.

"First story on the history series coming up," I told the weekend producer.

"No, that's next week," she said.

"No," I tried to contradict.

"Sorry." She shook her head.

"No?" This time I asked the "no," and at a much lower volume.

"Next Sunday."

"You're not kidding?" I asked.

She again shook her editorial head.

"And what do you have for tonight?" she asked.

"Tonight? Like in three hours?"

She didn't repeat the question.

"I'll go out and find something," I said, knowing my prayer to the story god was going to need a lot of exclamation marks.

I asked where the new young cameraman I was working with was now? I could meet him. We could start looking.

"He's been sent to another assignment," she said.

"Is anyone free?"

"No," she said.

I know she was thinking that I've had a cameraman all day and have nothing to show for it for tonight's news. But she was kind and she just said, "No."

Then she added, "But we do have one shooting a few seconds at the Japanese prayer service. You could have him afterwards."

Prayers for Japan? That is an answer for my prayers.

"When is he shooting it?" I asked.

"It started five minutes ago downtown. Good luck."

I got there at 4:25. It was due to be over at 4:30. You probably know that because of this city's insane government you still have to pay parking meters on Sundays. I dug desperately through my pockets and then through the book bag I have carried for thirty years. It usually has my lunch in it.

I found four quarters. One quarter for two and a half minutes. That's crazy. I put in four. That gave me ten minutes to do the story.

I ran across the street, met the cameraman, talked to three people in the back of the church and left while they were still singing a hymn.

Luckily there was one of the microwave trucks patrolling downtown. These are trucks that can broadcast from almost anywhere and have edit suites inside. To edit, the reporter sits on the front seat turned around backward while the editor sits on an office chair anchored by a bungee cord.

There are empty cups of Tim Hortons and Starbucks inside because that is the fuel that keeps the inside of the truck going.

I wrote and the editor put the pictures together, and he sent it over the air three minutes before it went back out on the air.

On the screen were a few crying faces, and many stoic ones. Hence a story about feeling and caring that was scheduled for a handful of seconds got the full treatment of a major story, which makes me think that it wasn't a mistake that I got the wrong date for the history series.

My friend who had earlier said we were putting too many crying people on the air said the story was very good. At least we put it in a church and not around piles of smashed houses.

He saw it his way:

"I just watched for a minute. But I said a prayer for them. They were hurt so bad and did so little complaining."

I didn't tell him he was part of the ratings. That was something that had no significance at all.

6

A Super New Unbelievable Recipe: Pancakes

Everyone is writing about food. Half the TV reality shows are now about food. Other bloggers on the Global website write about food. Everybody has the perfect recipe.

Well, actually, they don't. I do.

Every time our granddaughters spend a night with us I ask what they would like for breakfast. It is silly to ask because it is a ritual.

"Chocolate chip pancakes," says Ruby, who is seven. She has been saying this since she was five, or maybe four.

Her little sister Zoe can't talk yet, but when she hears "chocolate chip pancakes" she looks up from her toys and smiles. Then she tottles—that's a word that means the action of someone whose concept of walking is better than their talent for it—she tottles to the doorknob that has her bib hanging on it.

"We better cook quick," says Ruby.

The neatest thing about chocolate chip pancakes is you need someone to help you make them, ideally someone who is seven.

"Put some flour in the bowl," I say.

"How much," she asks.

"Just the right amount, then a little more."

"Can I crack the eggs?" she asks.

"Crack away."

What is more fun than cracking an egg and then watching half of it slide down the outside of the bowl and no one is upset?

"How many?" she asks.

"Two and a half, the half you have there halfway into the bowl is perfect. How did you know we needed exactly two and a half? That's hard to do with an egg."

At this moment she is a very proud cook.

"Milk. How much milk? Ruby, how much milk?"

"Just the right amount and a little more," she says. She is catching on.

Zoe's face has flour on it. Somehow Zoe has found the flour. That is impossible because she is less than three feet tall and the flour is four feet up on a counter.

She must have super flour powers. All mothers know about this. Luckily her mother is still sleeping. She needs the sleep. She has two small children.

Zoe tries to lick the flour off her face. Ugh. She doesn't like flour.

Back to the pancakes. Now we're adding oatmeal. That makes it healthy.

"How much oatmeal?" asks Ruby.

"A handful. My handful. That means two of your handfuls."

She counts.

"Add sugar," I say.

"How much?" I say before she can ask.

"Just a little and a little more," says Ruby.

Of course she knows not to add too much sugar, because the magic ingredient is still to come.

A pinch of salt is fun.

"What's a pinch?"

"This much, exactly," I say holding up a pinch, more or less. "But remember, your pinch is less than my pinch and your pinch is more than Zoe's pinch. That's something about life. When someone tells you something you may not always know what they are talking about."

It's the kind of lesson you don't find in either public or Sunday school.

"And baking powder. A teaspoon."

"My teaspoon, or Zoe's, or yours?" Ruby asks.

She has already learned the lesson.

"You choose, and then double it. That will make them nice and fluffy."

Some oil—got to have oil or you can't eat them.

How much? Again, just the right amount.

Then the secret ingredient. "What goes in chocolate chip pancakes that is still missing?" I ask.

Ruby smiles and asks, as she always does, can she have some without putting them into the batter?

I answer, as I always do, "That's why we're making the pancakes."

She puts some in the bowl and a few in her mouth and more in the bowl, and a few more in her mouth. Somewhere in the recipe that is enough.

Then fry, trying to make Mickey Mouse heads in the pan and failing, and then eating.

"You want syrup?" I ask.

"No, these are perfect," she says, being the best food critic I know.

And Zoe and Ruby have breakfast. In sixty years they will repeat it for some other little ones and the measurements will be exactly the same.

Chasing a Bus

Your perception of reality can change in an instant. That is a fancy way of saying we really don't know what we want. Or at least I don't.

Earlier today a cameraman and I saw a fellow suddenly start running for a bus. It was a block and a half away. That was wishful thinking, I thought, but we all have that.

The fellow was one of those kind of leftover hippies with long hair, those skinny vegetarian types who are anti-establishment, with a trendy one-shoulder knapsack on his back. My first thought was you are trying to look like you are in the '60s, but that's when your parents were born.

That has nothing to do with catching a bus, but having lived through the '60s and once upon a time having been slimmer and having long hair, and once for a full day having given up meat, I thought, "Get your own identity and leave my past to me, fellow." You see how easy it is to have prejudice?

My second thought was that if he makes it almost to the bus and the driver sees him and is kind, he will keep the driver and

41

passengers waiting. That's not nice. Why should he slow them down? So I was half hoping he would miss it by a long distance. That wouldn't put the driver in a dilemma.

And besides, no one could reasonably expect to run that far and that fast. I couldn't do it, and so therefore he shouldn't. That makes sense.

Also he had 49th Avenue to cross and the light was against him. That would mean he'd be a criminal, or dead, so why try? I mean, I would wait for the next bus. And where are you going that's so important anyway, fellow?

There were still two more passengers in line waiting to get on the bus and he had a block to go. Never, I thought. Impossible. I didn't add, "Ha ha," because that would be cruel, but have you ever wished someone would be stopped by the next red light just because his car was too fancy? Okay, if you haven't you are a good person.

The cameraman, Randy Mennie, and I were stuck in traffic on Main Street, and after commenting on the weather we had run out of things to talk about. So we watched.

The runner was now in the middle of 49th Avenue. He was dodging cars. Whooh, that was close. An angry horn. Another. He was still crossing the street and the last person was climbing onto the bus. Now I was rooting for him. Now he had a chance. He was not quitting.

"Go fellow, go," I said out loud. I don't know why I said it, but the words were coming out and hitting the windshield.

"He just might make it," said Randy. He said it like he had money riding on him, like he was rooting for him.

The runner was on the track. We were in the grandstands.

Ninety feet to go, the same as tearing down the baseline from home plate to first base after you've hit the ball to the short stop. It's impossible. You can't make it. No one makes it.

Go fellow, go, I'm thinking. You can do it. I am hoping with all my heart that he gets that bus. No other bus will do.

Thirty feet, about one bus length to go to the rear bumper, and the driver closed the door. Twenty feet and the blinker was on. Ten feet and the runner lunges forward and slaps the side of the bus near the back door just as the big metal box starts to move.

Stop, I'm yelling inside my head. This guy is now my hero.

The blinker goes off. The driver has a golden heart. Now it doesn't matter to me that the passengers have to wait a few seconds longer. They are at the rail at the end of the race. They get to ride with someone who deserves their admiration. He has done what we all try to do, he has caught the bus. Randy slaps the dashboard. "Nice run."

"You got all that on tape, right?" I say. His camera is locked away in a burglar-proof box behind us.

He laughs. But that's all it takes to bring ourselves a real life story, just a moment of real life.

A psychological thriller with a chase scene and a change of attitude in the audience and a surprise, happy ending, all in 45 seconds.

And one last bit of reality. If he'd been wearing sandals, as we all did in the '60s, instead of sneakers, he would be waiting for the next bus.

Okay, Let's Get Down
to the Absurd

This is crazy. Totally crazy. Seven books by someone who was a Sweathog.

You remember *Welcome Back, Kotter*? If you smiled, thank you. That was a super sit-com during the 1970s about a dedicated New York City schoolteacher in a class of rejects. It was based on an actual New York City classroom.

This was before political correctness grabbed the throat of ordinary humans and turned them into non-thinking bubble heads. (The first time I wrote that I said Babble Heads. That is probably more correct.)

The *Welcome Back, Kotter* class was not one but many classes spread across the city.

If you were smart and did well in school and you were in grade 12, you were assigned to class number 12-1. Those were the kids going to university who would become doctors and lawyers, or drug addicts from too much demand being placed on them. If you were still smart enough to read and showed up on time for school but couldn't get into 12-1, you would go into 12-2 or 12-3. Your mother would try to hide the shame, because you would still get into a place of higher education but you might not get a scholarship, which meant she would have to dig up the money to pay for you until you stopped having fun in college and got a job to pay your own way.

Less bright kids would go to 12-4 or 12-5. They would graduate, but no one bragged about it. Then there were 12-6 and 12-7 kids. They went to work in gas stations or warehouses. And so the numbers fell like rain on a Vancouver day in autumn or spring or winter or summer until you got to, oh no. You cannot put my son in that class! Not that one!! Please. What will the neighbours say? What will I say? He can't be that bad.

Yup. 12-13. You can't get lower than 12-13. The class of Sweathogs. We weren't called Sweathogs. That term was created by the writer who created the series. It is a perfectly accurate descriptive name. The good thing about good writing or good talking is that when you find a juicy word to explain what you are talking about, you get your meaning across. Bingo. I can see what you mean. Sweathogs. Dummies, but smelly, too. Work on a word yourself. It is more fun than crossword puzzles. When you get a good word you get your meaning across.

On the other hand, if you hear something on television or read something and you find your mind wandering, it is usually not your fault. Television newsrooms are crowded with pretty people who have no idea how to describe what is in front of their eyes. They are more concerned with looking as though they know what they are talking about, which is a phenomenal talent also pursued professionally by politicians.

Anyway, we weren't called anything. If we had been, it would have been Losers, but that all-consuming worn-out term hadn't yet been invented. We were just the ones down the hall, the kids in the last classroom. We had to pass the kids in the other rooms on our way to ours. We made fun of them. What else could you do?

Inside the classroom there were no maps on the walls or diagrams of algebraic solutions. There was just the one poor teacher who was assigned here and who knew that he (and it was always a he—they would never put a woman into this class) had nowhere else to go. Education was not his goal. His instructions to us consisted of "Shut up" followed by "I told you to shut up." Being repeated endlessly, it eventually sank in and we did sometimes shut up, between outbursts.

There were 12-13s in every school, and that's why it could be turned into a multi-gazillion dollar television show that was instantly understood. In the show the students were witty, lovable misfits. That was the work of a writer. The teachers would have said, "That's absurd and ridiculous. The students were losers, the kind of kids who hated school, hated after school, and didn't particularly like anything that was associated with anything else, which included everything."

Are you wondering whether this all self-absorbed talking is about me? No, actually, it's not. As some others of you may be figuring out, this is about your kids, too, or your neighbour's kids. You or someone else reading this is saying, "That's my son or daughter. That's her, a loser. (You should use a more imaginative word.) I am embarrassed by her and she is driving me to suicide."

Rule number one: Don't kill yourself. Two: Don't kill the kid. Keep breathing, wait and hope, but most of all just wait. You never know what will happen. I was there.

These same kids have been around since kids were invented. They are created by an endless list of excuses from bad breakfast cereal to mothers who have to go to work.

Now they are in alternative schools, completely separated

from other kids. It is still 12-13 and it is funny that in a society that promotes inclusion of kids with physical and mental problems, even putting them on billboards and on television, kids with social problems are segregated. On the other hand they now have teachers who grew up watching *Welcome Back, Kotter* and who believe they can help them. If you ever pray for someone, secretly so no one sees you, and even if you don't believe in anything, pray for them. Those teachers deserve it, and they need it.

Back to me. "Shut up. Yes, you, jerk. I told you to shut up."

That was the lesson for the day.

Okay. I can wait until 3 p.m. when I can go to the taxicab garage where I worked pumping gas into a fleet of seventy cabs that pulled in between 3 and 6 p.m. Me and one other guy who was always on the other side of the pumps and we never got to know each other. But it was there that I met real people who drove all day and smoked even though the sign said "No Smoking" while I shoved the gas nozzle into the hole in their fender. Then I opened their hood and checked their oil and checked the fluid levels in their batteries and then the water in the radiator. That was scary, especially in the summer when everything overheated. I would put a towel over the cap on the sizzling radiator and pray, please don't blow up, please. Sometimes my prayers were not heard. That would mean a lot of boiling water shooting through my monkey suit and through my shirt and onto my stomach. I had a flat stomach then, which I sucked in every time I checked a radiator. It was good exercise. If I did that now I wouldn't be fat.

And I listened to the cabbies who'd dropped out of school in 9-13 and 10-13 tell me about the couple who were smooching in the back of their cabs. Smooching is as far as the description went, and it was a good word. I could picture it, even if I had never smooched in the back of a cab. I had a picture in my head while I was closing the gas cap on his cab. And I heard about the riders who tried to jump out without paying. All the cabbies carried a tire iron next to them on the front seat. The thieves seldom got out the back door before they were facing the iron bar in an extremely angry cabby's hand.

And there were the drunks in the back seat who couldn't get the window down in time. Every story was exciting or touching or disgusting.

Then after sweeping out the massive garage at 7 p.m. I walked home, still smelling of gasoline. It was hard to do homework, so I didn't.

But in school I started reading the newspapers that the teachers brought into 12-13. It wasn't the *New York Times* or the *Wall Street Journal*. The teachers assigned to these classrooms read the tabloids, including the *New York Daily News*, the papers that were written on the level of a sixth grader and concentrated on crime and scandal. Most of the stories were three paragraphs long. An in-depth feature would be six paragraphs.

I couldn't read well. To call myself dyslexic is cheating. The words are all jumbled when I look at them, the letters are mixed up when I write them, even now, but dyslexia hadn't been invented when I was in school. "Doesn't read well" was the diagnosis, and 12-13 was the solution.

Nonetheless, I could get through three paragraphs, given enough time, and in 12-13 I had all day. Instead of text books I had the tabloids of the teachers who said, "Shut up."

What I read about were the famous Mafia criminals—Two Finger Maloney was my favourite—and a couple just married riding a motorcycle around the world. Those were the same stories as the cabbies told, and even to me in the world of "Shut Up" it was obvious those stories were the world of newspapers.

"What do you want to do when you eventually get out of school?" my mother asked.

"Work for a newspaper." What else could there be?

In the middle of February 1962, I got out of school. You notice it was not June, and it wasn't quite a graduation. It was an exiting.

My mother didn't make the official goodbye—she was working—but she did buy a six pack of beer and two ham sandwiches to celebrate.

"What do you want to do now?" she asked.

"Work for a newspaper," I said. I had this down pat by now.

"Well, then you should go to a newspaper," she said.

She wasn't blinded by impossibility. She gave me a subway token. One token. She didn't expect me to come back.

If you already know this story then you've read my first book, and for that I thank you. Most of you, statistically, extrapolating from the numbers sold, have not. Many people tell me "I read your book and I liked it."

"One book?"

"Do you have another?"

What am I to say? What about the others? I can't do that. That would sound arrogant, and that I am not, I hope. I say thank you. But I know that most of you reading these books don't know I can't actually read. I struggle through a press release in the office and ten minutes later have no idea what it was about. Unless there are meaningful words in the writing and some action about Two Finger Maloney or a lost cat, I can't follow it. And if it has "therefores" and "in consideration ofs" in a sentence, I have no idea what it is talking about.

If you read Book One, *Chasing the Story God*, you know some of this. And if you did then I owe you an apology. I figure I should pay you back, so if you already know I can't read and that I write books and write for television while I can't write a clear sentence then send me a self-addressed stamped envelope and I will return a reasonable portion of the purchase price of this book, to be calculated by me (but you should be aware I didn't do well in math either).

However, if you have gained the idea that your own child who is floundering in school can do better and will be a shining light in your eye, then the deal is off. The premise of this book, of all my writings, of all my life, is "Things will get better. Just don't give up."

I can type. I can close my eyes and tell myself what I want to say and I write it. Just please don't ask me later to read it out loud.

Anyway, the morning after I got out of high school I rode a subway train to Times Square. I had heard the *New York Times* was there. I went upstairs and into the personnel office.

It was a very formal office, because the *New York Times* is a very formal newspaper.

"I would like to apply for a job as a copy boy," I said. I knew copy boys were the bottom of the ladder for working in a newspaper.

"We have an opening for an outdoor messenger," the nice man said.

I left. It wasn't the messenger part that bothered me, but it was February and have you ever been in Ottawa or Montreal or Toronto or Dawson City or Whitehorse in the winter? New York is worse. It has the cold plus the traffic. If you get hit by a bus at 20 below it hurts.

I walked across the city to the East River thinking I could throw my failure of a self into the water when I saw a mural on the front of a building across the street. It had pictures of people, many people, and a sign above it saying, "He Made So Many Of Them."

It sounded like the Bible. I liked it. It is at 220 East 42nd Street. If you go to New York on a trip, you can still see it. I crossed the street and only then saw a sign that said it was the *New York Daily News*, one of those papers that I had read in the classroom of 12-13. I hadn't looked up the *Daily News* address beforehand. I had only one location in mind, Times Square. After that it was a hot dog stand and home to the taxi garage.

Instead this was another newspaper. I took the elevator to the personnel department on the fourth floor.

"I want to be a copy boy," I said.

No one paid any attention to me.

"Can I apply for a job?" I asked.

No one even looked up. They were all listening to the radio, and when you listened to the radio back then, and it was important, you would bend your head down close to the box. John Glenn was circling the earth. He was the first American in space to go all the way around and come back to the starting line. The story, in living hold-your-breath reality, was live on the radio.

"Yes?" a man said to me, but he didn't look up from the radio.

You notice it was a man? When I started it was all men all the time. Now, on a typical day, the men in the Global newsroom are about 30 percent. As I keep saying, if you are a woman, or a minority, or someone in 12-13, hang in there. Your time is close.

"I want to be a copy boy," I said.

He didn't look at me. "Here, fill this out," he said.

He gave me a piece of paper. I struggled to fill in my name and address. I handed it back to him.

He glanced at it and put it in the In box. "You can start Monday in the mail room," he said. Then he went back to the radio.

Everyone was worried that John Glenn would die, would burn up coming back through the earth's atmosphere. We would have a burned-toast astronaut in space. Seriously, everyone was deeply concerned.

Everyone except me. I had no idea anyone was in space. I didn't buy a newspaper while looking for a job in a newspaper.

There was no interview, no evaluation. I had a job, thanks to an astronaut who did land safely and a mural that I didn't know was there. Eleven years later I was a veteran of prison riots, shootings, stabbings, kidnappings and other occurrences of the night, and I left the newspaper and New York for Vancouver.

If you know this story already you can get your money back, as I said, at a rate determined by me, but no matter what you do: Don't give up on your own kid. You never know what will happen.

P.S. The fellow who created *Welcome Back, Kotter*, Gabe Kaplan, was a student in one of those classes. He also played the part of the teacher who came back. And he wrote most of the stories. The lesson is obvious. Don't say you can't do it just because everyone calls you stupid. And don't give up on your kids even if they act that way. They are just getting ready for a life that you don't expect—possibly a life of outstanding excellence, maybe even in television.

Money in the Mud

It is ridiculous to think that God had anything to do with it. God was busy splitting atoms and making other universes.

My wife and I were driving down a dried mud road behind a long stretch of blackberries in the Deep South. It was hot and we were hungry. We were not happy. Hunger and heat can ruin your day.

When I wasn't looking for blackberries I was defending the United States of America, having been assigned to an air base that was supposed to protect America from a missile attack from Cuba.

It was hot in Cuba that day, too, and they had the same old junky vintage Chevrolet that I was driving. Countries about to go to war with each other should really get to know each other first. If we talked about pistons and patching mufflers, wars would probably be unnecessary.

I had paid $150 for the car, which had no floor. My wife put her feet up on the hump over the transmission and I kept mine on the pedals and we watched the ground go by underneath as we drove. It was challenging.

I had to have a car because we were living off the air base in a tiny shack on the edge of an old, empty trailer court. We were doing that because we were married and had a baby and we chose to be together. She could have stayed with her parents a thousand miles away and I could have lived in the barracks on the base but you know what happens when you are in love.

"You are crazy, boy."

They say that a lot in the South. White or Black, you are Boy unless you have drunk enough alcohol in your life to have sagging jowls. In the South there were many with sagging jowls who were not Boys. They were Old Boys, with sagging jowls.

Crazy because I still had to report at 6 a.m. on the base. Crazy because no one would wake me at 5 a.m. with a musical rendition of Reveille piped in on the speakers in the barracks.

Crazy because no one would make breakfast for me in the mess hall.

Crazy because how do I get to the base? Before the car I had to hitchhike, at 5:30 a.m.! That alone was crazy.

Crazy because I could no longer eat in the mess hall at all. I gave up that right, and had to live on $100 a month, which is crazy. That was the basic pay of a soldier with one stripe in the 1960s.

So my wife and I were not getting fat. Half the money went for rent. Half for baby food.

So we were out picking blackberries and, as I say, it was hot. The road was dried mud with two deep ruts.

"There are better berries back there," said my wife.

We had already been back there, I thought. Move ahead, always move ahead.

"We should go back," she said.

And thus begins what you would call an argument. This way or that, it doesn't take much to find something to argue about, not when the weather is bad and life is miserable.

But I would show her. I would go back. I got back in the car, started it, put it in reverse and stepped on the gas—hard. That would show her.

Then I stopped and got out and watched her walking back down the dried mud road toward me. I had backed up just like she wanted. I had obeyed. I had followed the most dumb order in the world. Who would believe blackberries would be better here than up there? But I'd show her.

I got out and walked around to the back of the car, because back there the berries would be better, for sure. Only I could show her they weren't.

Love is miserable when it comes to arguments.

I got behind our car and looked down. Right behind the bumper, directly below it, stuck in the dried mud, were two twenty dollar bills half sticking up.

They weren't under the car, which they would have been if I had gone another six inches. They were not ten feet behind it and unnoticeable, which they would have been if I had stopped one second earlier.

They were on their edges, sticking straight up, half out of the mud. They were curled a bit so that they each made a sort of half-circle.

"Don't stop walking," I said to my wife, who had stopped at the front of the car to pick berries. "Please come here."

I didn't get the "Why?" She came. I pointed down. We looked at each other, and then looked down again.

How do you say Impossible, Unbelievable or This can't be? How do you say any of those disbelieving words? You don't. You look at each other and then look around to see if it is a joke, but you know that's impossible because this is a single-lane back road with bushes on both sides between nowhere and nowhere.

We pulled the bills out of the mud and drove into town. This was before McDonald's, if you can believe such a time existed, but there was a hamburger stand in the middle of town. It sold the World's Largest Hamburgers, 19 inches around, which meant they were a sixteenth of an inch thick with a lot of bread.

We bought two—each.

Meanwhile, God was off making another universe, so that had nothing to do with it. We were just lucky.

10

Another Strange Route
to a Good Destination

To say life is prearranged is stupid. At least it is to me. When someone says something was meant to be, I think, "No. Nothing was meant to be. That would make us puppets."

If things are meant to happen then what is the point of us doing anything? If everything is prearranged, we are hanging on the end of a string and the play is already scripted.

You get hit on the head with a frying pan by the woman who owns the apple tree that you have just tried to steal apples from. You have strings attached to your arms. You couldn't help stealing the apples. The woman with the frying pan has strings on her arms, too. Bong.

The kids in the audience laugh because this is a comedy on a stage and you are made of wood and someone is pulling the strings.

Except:

A nice man called me and said he had all my books. Bless him. And he liked them. Bless him even more. Would I sign them? Of course, certainly, almost right away.

He lived in Point Grey. Rich folks. I told him I hardly ever go there because rich folks don't often come out of their homes to putter in their yards. They are at work making more money, which is good for the economy, but not for me when I'm trying to find someone to photograph while they are doing something I think is interesting.

I hang around Main Street instead. There are lots of people there. But as for signing his books, you bet, you got it. I'll be there as soon as I can.

And then I lost his name. No matter where I looked it was not there. I have many notes because my life is a series of wonderful people and I don't want to forget them. So I take notes. Some I scribble on the back of a receipt from the grocery store because that's the only thing in my pocket. Some I write on the back of a business card, often one I got from the last person I met. Some go in the official Reporter's Notebooks that they give me at work.

So I have everything I need.

Except I cannot find the note with the name of the nice man who wants me to sign his books. Remember, these are ALL my books that he has. He is the kind of reader I pray for. And if you who are reading this have all of them, you too are the answer to my prayers. You and he are supporting Variety. Plus, the nice man on the phone told me he has read all of them. It will be an honour to sign them. But I cannot find his name.

Time passes. I think of him every day. I look for the note and I feel bad. I know that he is thinking the same as I would think; this bum said he would come by but three months have passed and he hasn't. He hasn't even called.

Six months, and I am still feeling bad.

Now let's go back ten years to a different story.

I hear about the Morris Men doing a medieval dance in a

park. They do it at sunrise, at 5:51 a.m. on May 1st. I heard about this ten years ago and arranged for a cameraman to meet me.

It was 6 a.m. when my phone rang. "Are you coming?" It was the cameraman.

"No. Can't be. Now?" That was all followed by another pathetic "Nooooo!", trying to find forgiveness for sleeping when I should have been working.

I've had ten years to learn about the Morris Men.

Briefly, they are wonderful nutcases who dance for the sun and the moon and the goddess of fertility. In truth, if you have enough sun and moon with the right person you usually have fertility. That is the way nature wisely works with the goddess of fertility.

When two people spend a warm day under the sun followed by a warm evening looking up at the moon, the arrival of children later is not an accident. Those are the strings held by nature and the goddess of, of course, fertility.

The Morris Men have been doing their thing since the 1400s in England. That was before television and so they danced because, well, what else are you going to do if you can't watch Donald Trump and *Survivor*? They do this in the dead of awful winter on December 21st when the nights are the longest. No one comes out to watch them then because it is cold and raining and miserable, but they do it because they are dedicated—and crazy.

They also do it on May 1st, because May Day is warm and the sun comes up early. They click sticks together and wave scarves and listen to a concertina, an old-fashioned accordion with no buttons that is much more fun than an accordion.

Just a side note. When I was young I saw someone playing an accordion and worried about him. He was sitting down and squeezing this big box over his lap. I had once gotten my penis caught in the zipper of my pants and there is still no pain, even death by guillotine, that could come close to that. I worried about the accordion player, but a concertina is small and user friendly, even if the user is a man sitting down.

Over the following decade I promised myself some day that I would see the Morris Men again and put them on television.

Then I met Irene, who is the caretaker of Trimble Park in Vancouver. She was decorating a little monkey tree she had planted in the park with Easter eggs. She did it for the kids in the nearby school. That is kind and sweet. She wound up on television.

She grew up on a native reserve in Saskatchewan with thirteen brothers and sisters in a small, cold three-bedroom house.

Lesson: Don't complain about your life.

She and her husband, a retired Mountie who rides a motorcycle, care for the park, care for each other and are nice.

She told me that the Morris Men have a ceremony on May 1st on the basketball court in the park. I should come and see it. They also have a horse.

I will. I set the alarm clock. I cannot sleep because I am afraid of not hearing it.

The alarm clock rang at 4 a.m. Please understand this is the night after the Canucks second game with Nashville. The game went to a double overtime. The Canucks lost, in the last minute of the double overtime.

I repeat double overtime because it was very late. The cameraman assigned to work with me had already gone to bed because he is smart. He knew he had to get up at 4 a.m.

After the Canucks lose my wife said something about needing help cleaning out a closet. I am too old and too wise to question what a wife needs.

An hour later we went to bed. Three hours later the alarm went off.

We got to the park before the sun was up. The cameraman, Karl Cassleman, whom you read about in the last book, lives for eating and drinking coffee and joking and making life into a dessert. He said he was stopping for donuts and coffee for us because getting up at this hour was as dumb as can be.

He arrived, just on time, and together we did the story of the Morris Men dancing to bring up the sun on May 1st. Without them it would not have come up. Forget what was taught to you in school about the earth spinning and that is why the sun rises. That may be true the rest of the year, but not on May 1st.

The Morris Men have been helping the sun rise for 600 years. You don't argue with success.

They danced and sang and the sun came up, the same as it did in the year 1400 in tiny villages in England. Why did the sun come up? It would have anyway, right?

On the other hand, do you want to take that chance?

They danced and the cold night air melted under the morning sun and everyone was happy and the fertility horse, which was a man under a puppet horse head, went around trying to nibble on every woman who was watching. He went to some sweet little old ladies who came close to smacking him across the snout. Rule number one: You do not mess with the psyches of little old ladies.

And then it was over. Everyone was happy, the story was fine and Karl the cameraman said, as he always does, "Let's eat!"

White Spot wasn't far away. White Spot is another way to spell "how to make a million dollars by just opening your eyes and putting two and two together."

A fellow named Nathan Bailey in Vancouver knew young people liked two things, besides other young people. They liked hamburgers, of course—even in 1928 that was the food of choice—but they also liked cars, mostly their Model T Fords souped up and filled with young people.

Nat scraped together enough to buy a vacant lot at 67th and Oak Street. It was outside the city limits back then. It was cheap. It was basically a parking lot. Perfect. Parking lots were where you put cars.

He built a tiny burger shack in a corner of the lot. It had a few small tables, but he didn't need them. His working tables were long trays that stretched across the seats of the cars that were pulling into his lot. The trays hooked onto the windows and a new way of life was born.

Kids with cars, families with kids in the back seat of their cars and those who wanted to be part of this neat new way of eating all lined up to get into the parking lot.

This was not a drive-through, like McDonald's. This was "Let's drive over to the drive-in and meet the guys and get a burger and shake."

Nat became rich. The name, White Spot, by the way, was lifted from a restaurant in California where the car and burger culture was invented, but they have never complained so don't tell them.

And the famous Triple O (you probably know this) was a locally created name that became a signature. When a thing has a catchy name sales usually go up.

"Give me a burger with mayo, lots of mayo and pickles, and tomatoes."

The waitress wrote "B" on the order slip for burger and "O" for mayo, which became the special secret sauce, "OO" for mayo and pickles, and "OOO" for the works: tomatoes, lettuce, pickles and special sauce, for no extra charge. You can't pass up that. It didn't take long before the trendy teens would drive to the White Spot to get a Triple O.

Nowadays most of us can't wait to get out of our cars, but many of us still go to White Spot and Triple O's are still their mainstay.

After the Morris Men, I ordered bacon and eggs. Karl wanted the Grand Slam. That would be a snack to keep him going following the donuts and coffee he got on the way to the park in the morning, until more donuts about 10 a.m. to keep him going until lunch. He carries 25 pounds of camera on his shoulder and when he works he moves like the wind in a storm around and through the scene he is filming. If he stopped eating, television news would have blank spots.

But there was a problem. It was 6:30 a.m. and although White Spot was open it did not have cooks who were awake. We got coffee and time passed. Karl talked about having steaks for dinner. I said I was hoping for Chinese take-out. More time passed.

The nice waitress said they were a little backed up.

A guy at a table in front of me got tired of waiting and left. I felt bad for him. It is an empty feeling to have an appetite and be forgotten.

We waited. Half an hour later Karl saw a couple of cooks just showing up, still rubbing their eyes and obviously late. It happens.

It didn't matter. We talked, about office gossip and vacations and kids and grandkids, and Karl got a text on his phone. He should get to the next assignment, the plant sale at VanDusen Garden. I usually do a story on that, because the people who shop there are dedicated gardeners, but they are crazy.

They spend hundreds of dollars for plants with long names that come in small pots. For some people there's competition in the garden for "my plant has a longer Latin name than your plant."

But they are supporting VanDusen, which I think is wonderful. VanDusen Garden is an amazing place if you want to learn something about unusual plants, and the one day a year to go there is during their plant sale when admission is free. You don't have to buy plants, so go and look at them.

But Karl cannot go because we are still waiting for our breakfasts.

At a table in front of me a tall, thin, grey-haired man settled in. He ordered just as we were getting our meals.

With the cooks at work, the tall thin man who had just sat down got his eggs without delay. We ate. He ate. He looked at me as we got ready to leave.

He stopped me and asked if I was me and straight away I knew. I knew even before I nodded. I knew as soon as he spoke. Maybe it was his voice. Maybe it was some invisible string pulling my memory. Whatever it was, honest to God, the super God, I knew who he was.

"I called you," he said, but before he could finish his sentence I said, "You want me to autograph your books." I didn't even bother hoping I was right. I knew I was right. In front of me was the lost note with skin and breath and a smile.

"Yes," he said. "How did you know?"

"I don't know," I said. "I felt it."

His name is Fred Mah. He gave me his address, which was in Point Grey, not far from the White Spot.

In his living room he said he thought I might have lost his name or forgotten. He was forgiving and patient. I am lucky.

I signed all his books. He had all of them—amazing—and two copies of several of them because he was given them for Christmas. I was happy. I ran out of things to write in the books and he said, "Just put your name in them." He was kind.

How did that happen? How come we had to wait for our eggs and pancakes until Fred arrived?

Then Fred told me he hadn't gone to that White Spot in months. It was just a whim to go that morning.

How come I met Irene who told me about the Morris Men?

How come I didn't do a story on them ten years earlier?

How come the cooks were late?

There are no strings. It wasn't meant to be. It is impossible and dumb to think that it was. It was sheer coincidence. I would never believe anything else.

I went home. My wife said she wasn't in the mood for Chinese take-out. She wanted something simple. I said I could make some shrimp and macaroni.

She liked that. She went into the garden because she had been at the VanDusen plant sale with our daughter and our granddaughters and she had plants to put into our garden. She told me they had impressive names in Latin.

I put the macaroni and water on the stove. I was tired. I lay down on the bed and put my head on a pillow.

I knew nothing else until I heard the phone ringing. I got up, groggy. Smoke was coming into the bedroom. It filled the kitchen. On the phone was my neighbour asking if our house was on fire. The pot of macaroni looked and smelled like the top of an exploding volcano.

I threw it into the sink, opened the windows and door and answered the front door for my neighbour, who was offering a fan.

Then I called the local Chinese restaurant and ordered take-out.

It was delicious, it was just what I wanted, but don't tell me anything about "It was meant to be."

11

My Wife Told Me to Straighten Up

I told my wife that I had just written a blog on the Global website about the man who had taken over Gerry's spot on the approach to the Ironworker's Bridge.

I was annoyed at him. He has the right to be there, but Gerry had made that a holy place. For ten years he had waved at drivers and never asked for a handout.

He said nice things to everyone who passed by and he picked up litter—mostly cigarette butts. He smiled and waved and complimented and cheered up the day for tens of thousands.

On Valentine's Day he put red hearts on the little concrete island he walked on. The island was a heavily sloped road divider and very difficult to walk on, but Gerry did it all day long—again, for ten years.

At Christmas he put a branch on the island and decorated it.

When a traffic sign was knocked down he put up a replacement made from stolen pieces of lumber from a construction site and hi-vis tape. I don't know where he got that from, but I know he carried the lumber by bus from the west end to the east side.

Gerry was wonderful. Then he died.

His sons in Winnipeg had thought he was a heroin addict begging on East Hastings and sleeping in alleyways. They had forbidden their grandchildren from learning anything about him.

Then he died and they were contacted and came to the funeral.

The funeral home donated their building because the director liked Gerry. A minister donated her services because Gerry always said sweet things to her.

The funeral home was filled with suit-wearing people who had been moved by Gerry, along with street people and jockeys from the track where Gerry donated the coins that he was given.

I gave the eulogy. I liked Gerry, a lot. His sons cried.

Then an imposter took over Gerry's island. He waved. He was not Gerry.

I wrote a blog that said: Get Off Gerry's Island. I told my wife.

"Why are you writing about someone begging for money when it is Christmas? You should be writing about Christmas things, like happy people and people doing good things."

Then she continued: "You should be writing about the lights and the good feeling that people have and the beautiful trees in our friend's houses. And you should talk about how happy kids get and the looks on their faces when they say Santa is coming. And while you're at it you should be writing about all the good Christmas songs that are so wonderful to listen to."

I started to nod, but then she went on: "You could be writing about how crowded churches get on Christmas Eve and at least on one night everyone is doing what they say they mean to do all year."

I tried to say I would but she said, "Don't put it off. You can't put off good things. You have to do what is important right away, otherwise it will look like it's not important to you."

I started to move my head up and down when she added, "I don't want to tell you what to write, but please, for everyone's sake, say Christmas, and say Merry, and at least once say God Bless Everyone."

Thank you. There is nothing left to say.

Except that she is right. God bless the new man on Gerry's island.

12

A New Home for Ruby

We finished the roof just before bedtime. That was good because Little One needed to sleep and all the noise of construction had to be finished.

I put down my last tool and Ruby said the roof was crooked. She was right. We adjusted the roof.

Her first house, all her own, and she was happy.

It had two floors and an attic, which was the right size now. There was a combination living and dining room downstairs next to the kitchen. Upstairs there were two bedrooms and above that the attic, which was designed to be high enough to stand in as well as store everything that didn't fit downstairs.

Ruby said she would start painting the next day, or the next week when she came back for a visit. She then put on her coat, her mother picked up her baby sister and they went out to the car together.

Her new home was in our basement waiting for the glue on the roof to dry. She didn't want to take it home with her until it was all finished. We had been working on it for three weeks, or three visits, a total of about four hours of construction.

She wanted a house for her dolls after her mother had told her that Grandpa, that's me, had made her one when she was the same age as Ruby was now, grade one.

That was the year we moved to Canada.

We were broke after the move. That is not a surprise or a complaint. Most people spend most of their lives without enough money and it often happens after a major event, like quitting your job, renting a truck and moving your family from the Atlantic Ocean to the Pacific Ocean without knowing a soul on the Pacific side. And then starting a new job and finding an inexpensive duplex to live in with some pot-smoking kids living next door.

It was almost Christmas time and we had no money. That also happens to most people. In fact, many famous stories are written about such things. Usually the poor person gives the only thing that he or she has and it turns out to be the perfect gift. When the little trinket is unwrapped the starlight falls on it and makes it shine like gold. That's the way the stories have it, and sometimes it's true.

It was Christmas Eve, early in the day, and my daughter was hoping for a dollhouse. I went to a lumber yard. I had never been in a lumber yard in my life. I wasn't raised with a father or anyone who knew anything about building anything.

In the lumber yard I asked where there would be wood to make a dollhouse. Someone pointed to a stack of plywood. I bought a sheet and some nails and some brackets that I thought would hold the wood together and some screws. Then I bought a small handsaw and a screwdriver. That was all the money I had.

I couldn't get the sheet of plywood onto the roof of my car so I walked home holding it over my head. After the first block I thought I would never make it. A half-hour later I got home, five blocks away.

Then I walked back and got my car.

After dinner, when my son and daughter were sleeping, I went into the basement. I wanted to start by cutting out some walls, but when I tried to cut the wood the saw went off at an angle. I had never cut a piece of wood in my life.

I drew a line with a pencil and tried to follow it. That was impossible. The saw kept going that way, which was any way except the way I wanted it to go.

I held the saw very tightly and said it had to do this. The basement was cold. It was below ground. I cut one square, which wasn't really square. Then I cut another.

The night went on and the cold got deeper and I cut more. My wife asked if I was coming to bed. I said later. The cold was not nice. The shouting and the music next door stopped and I cut more squares. I tried to cut slowly because the saw was squeaking and I didn't want to make noise.

Sometime about when Santa was over Manitoba I had enough cut pieces. I tried to hold them together with glue, but you can't hold three walls up at the same time. I tried to screw in the brackets, but I had never screwed anything together before.

It was a funny kind of screwdriver I had bought. I didn't notice it in the lumber yard, but the end was square. I thought screwdrivers were straight. This was very easy to use but I had never seen one before anywhere in America.

Much later I learned that the square screwdriver was invented in Canada by a man whose invention led to a long, cold night like mine, but his lasted most of his life. P.L. Robertson dreamed up the idea of a square-ended screwdriver that tapered a bit. It fitted perfectly in the head of specially designed screws, didn't slip out and got the job done quickly.

But he had no money. So he went to England for financing. Someone there saw how good the idea was and he was happy to come up with the cash. The money fellow also saw how he could make more money by screwing poor Robertson out of his own screwdriver. He intentionally drove their little enterprise into bankruptcy and then bought the rights to the screwdriver from Robertson.

Robertson spent years trying to raise enough money to buy back the rights, which he did, and he said after that he would never part with them again.

You could hardly blame him. You would have done the same. Once you lose something you treasure and then get it back, you are not going to let it go again.

Except it was Henry Ford who wanted to buy Robertson's screwdriver the second time round so he could make Model Ts faster. Robertson said no.

Why do we take this long detour in the middle of making a dollhouse? Because we all make mistakes. Mostly they are caused by stubbornness and refusing to bend.

I knew I could make the dollhouse without any planning or preparation, without looking in any dollhouse-building books and without asking anyone in the lumber yard how to cut the wood.

I'm a guy. I can't ask something like that. What would they think? Anyway, I can cut the wood and put it together, easy. Except it was now 3 a.m. and I was freezing and I had pieces of wood around me on the floor and a square screwdriver.

Thankfully I could get the screws in. If the screwdriver had kept slipping out of the slot, as it would have if it was a plain old American-style slotted one, I wouldn't have been able to finish before Santa arrived.

I finished and the dollhouse, wrapped in newspaper with a

red ribbon on top, was under the tree just before Santa arrived. That was just minutes before a little girl woke up wondering if it was true, if Santa did come.

Robertson was not so lucky. He said no to Henry Ford, who told him that because of that his invention would never be used in America.

Even today you can hear in a hardware store in Alabama, "What's this, Bubba? A square screwdriver? Must be a commy plot."

To make Ruby's dollhouse we went to an arts and crafts store and bought pre-cut wood. Then we built it together. I held up the walls and she told me when they were straight. She put on the glue. We both held the roof until it was set enough to let go. Little One, her little doll, would now have a place to sleep.

"That's my last house," I told her just before she left.

"No," she said. "Zoe will need a house."

Right. Her little sister will have dolls, and she'll need a place for them to sleep.

In a few years I will get out the Robertson and some glue, but I will never, never buy a pre-made dollhouse, because a house without a story is not a home.

13

The Love Train

They were the nicest couple ever. He moved her ponytail out from where it was caught behind her chair.

"Thank you," she said to him. "It gets stuck there sometimes," she said to me.

Cerebral palsy, she had said to me earlier. That was why she was in a wheelchair.

"So you have never walked?" I asked her. This is one of those statements that pretends to be a question when you know the answer. Of course she has never walked. She has cerebral palsy. You can't walk when you have cerebral palsy, not a severe case of it, which Cathy had. Her legs wouldn't hold her even with crutches.

"No, never," she said. "But Ed and I have gone for many walks."

Ed was standing behind her looking like Santa Claus and smiling and Cathy's words were making my heart beat like the rat-a-tat-tat of a drum in a marching band. The words are strong and unbelievable and yet they are coming from a person who cannot walk. "We go for walks," said with a smile, and with tears.

74

My God, I am lucky. Sorry, that should be OMG, I am lucky. It's strange—there are some religions that kill you if you utter the name of their god and others that use their god as an exclamation mark. We really should sit down and talk about this.

Back to Cathy and Ed. They have been friends for twenty-five years. They met in church. He has been twice widowed. She has never been out of her chair, except when she is lifted into her bed.

They have a loyalty, a love, a companionship, a beauty that makes living a good experience, but I would have never known about them if cameraman Dave McKay hadn't been sent to a political press conference that morning. Dave is a neat guy. He is a nationally famous barbecue chef and a country music singer. He would look like one of the crowd in Texas. He wears cowboy boots when he is with me looking for a story at English Bay.

"Your first assignment," he was told early in the morning, "is at the Roundhouse in Yaletown. Some politician is going to say something about something and we have to be there." Then the assignment editor added, "Sorry."

A press conference with a politician is like chewing on glass. And the glass is even more cutting right before an election. It is painful, hard to swallow and basically a waste of time, but we have voted, or soon will vote, these people into power and so they have to flex their muscles, like teenagers in front of a mirror in a gym. The image they see differs from what is really there, but they believe they should periodically speak to the masses, and that is done through press conferences.

I don't know why we think a politician is smarter than any of the rest of us. I have met many before they were elected and they were just ordinary Jane and Joe schmucks. Some of them would have trouble telling the time on an old-fashioned watch with hands on it.

Then they get elected and they are suddenly in charge of our lives, our cities and our country. Poor us. And they have assistants who tell them the time.

So going to a press conference with one of those types isn't challenging. You set up your camera, you point it, you turn it on.

In your headset you hear that the other side is all wrong and this member of the side you are looking at knows all the answers. This side is right. This side knows what the people want. This side has listened to ordinary British Columbians. The other side has caused all the pain and suffering we have and never listens to ordinary British Columbians.

Vote this side.

Until you get to the next press conference, one for the other side. Different name. Same words.

But Dave hit a cameraman's pay dirt. After carrying his camera and tripod into the building he was told the press conference was rescheduled for the afternoon.

A normal human reaction to the cancellation of something you had carried supplies for would be, "What? Darn."

A cancelled political press conference gets, "Bless you."

He took a shortcut through the Roundhouse to get back to his truck. That change in direction was through the section of the building that has an old steam engine parked inside.

That didn't interest Dave, but a friendly fellow with a long, snow-white beard did.

"Hello," he said to Dave, "are you here about the train?" He had a smile. He had a twinkle in his eye. Dave knows good characters.

"No," he said. "Just politics."

The snow-white beard drooped. "Sorry," said the man behind it. He obviously wanted to talk about his train.

Dave was then assigned to work with me.

"I have found the neatest guy with a snow-white beard and he knows something about some train," he told me when we met up. He was so excited, and a country singing barbecue chef knows how to be excited.

Dave said the man with the beard was friendly. Dave said I would love him. I said, "Okay. Let's go," but Dave kept on telling me how wonderful he was. He didn't hear me because he knows I don't want to go to something that I know is there waiting for us. I want us both to find something and get excited and watch it happen right in front of us.

That is hard to explain, but it is the magic that not only makes the stories I do but also makes life fascinating. You find something such as a father hiding Easter eggs and you ask him why and he tells you it's because he had none when he was a child, or he tells you he always had them. In either case it's a discovery and suddenly you learn something about why he is doing that.

You have then expanded your universe.

But a snow-white beard is good enough for me and I know about the train Dave is telling me about and this is a good opportunity to do a story about it.

"Okay," I said.

"And you would love him," he said.

"OKAY. I like it. Let's go to the Roundhouse."

"I'm telling you, you'd like him," he said.

The wonderful thing about excitement is that it blocks out everything that is not exciting.

"Why don't we go to the Roundhouse?" I said.

"That's a good idea," he said.

Dave is so much smarter than me.

I was happy. As I've said every time I can say it, Vancouver has a past that is exciting. So much happened so quickly. A wilderness became a metropolis overnight—and much of it was because of that old steam engine in the Roundhouse.

"You know why that train's there?" I said to Dave.

"No."

"Don't you listen to my stories?" I asked.

"Sometimes, when I shoot them."

"Well, it's time you shot one on the famous 374. It's been on television before, but this time it will be wonderful because you are shooting it."

"What's 374?"

As we drove there I told him:

The old 374 is a massive hunk of black steel that sits quietly on a short section of railroad track.

It is the engine that made the first trip across Canada, in 1887, but more importantly, it is why British Columbia is not part of the US.

At the time, the good citizens of British Columbia were hacking down the forests and selling real estate as fast as the buyers were lining up, and the lines were long. Logging was highly profitable. The wood that came from here was gold. Even temples in China were being made out of BC logs. Some trees were 500 and 600 years old. You could get a beam 100 feet long that was five feet thick and had no knots in it. That was temple-building wood. That was beyond price. Of course, a hunk of lumber that long was a special order, only affordable by an emperor.

The only thing the hard-working Canadians of British Columbia did not have was a connection with the rest of Canada. All their dealings were either with the US or Asia.

"We should join the US," they said. They didn't mention that, at the same time, they were trying to keep Asians out. Those Oriental folks could buy wood, but please, just pick it up and leave.

America was appealing, mostly because it was there, right across the border—although few even knew where that was. There were no border lineups, no customs declarations, no hassle, no problems. This story is told more fully in Chapter 27, The Family Album.

The folks of British Columbia in the 1880s said either the eastern part of Canada had to put a train across the country so they could be part of that country, or they would join another country. They said it in many different words, but that about summed it up.

Here is where history gets tangled in political correctness. If you read the history books that are officially sanctioned you will learn that Eastern Canada wanted to hold onto Western Canada and had a train line built across the nation that was still not officially a nation. The train would bring the country together and everyone would be happy.

On the other hand there is the truth, or at least the most believable part of it. The Canadian Pacific Railway, which was a wild company of big, money-hungry and adventurous men, said, "They want a train to the Pacific? We will build them a train to the Pacific, and along the way we will claim all the land that we build through as ours. The people in the west will be happy and we will be rich. Let us correct that. We will be richer, much richer. After all, a rail line is just a way of delivering money into our bank accounts."

That is not in Canadian history books because it makes the cross-country trip seem less pure and holy. But the truth is basically that all human movement, all history, is driven by economic hunger. If we can make a buck we will go. The train came because the CPR made a profit from it.

When the folks in the little town on the west coast looked up they saw the smoke from the engine a mile away. It was burning wood. It came around the edge of Burrard Inlet from Port Moody. The train passed by what would later be the first Second Narrows Bridge, which was built before the First Narrows Bridge and before the current Second Narrows Bridge, which would later be renamed the Ironworkers Memorial Second Narrows Bridge, but at the time the train passed, in 1887, there were no bridges, just a wish by the eastern side of this country to hold onto the western side.

Back to the story. The smoke was rising and the people at Hastings Mill were cheering. The engine, number 374, arrived puffing steam from its pistons and smoke from its top stack. It was covered with cedar branches and banners that had been put on it in Port Moody.

The people said, okay, we will join Canada.

The engine was only one year old. It spent the rest of its life as a workhorse up and down the province and across the country. It was retired in 1945 and given to the city of Vancouver.

The first thing the CPR did was strip off all the modern additions that had been made to update the hard-working engine throughout its life. They made it look like it did on May 23, 1887.

The city put it on display in Kitsilano Beach on a short pair of tracks. It stood there for the next thirty-nine years. You may have climbed on it. My kids did. I thought it was a wonderfully Canadian thing, to let kids in a playground climb on a real old steam engine.

Before Expo '86 it was moved indoors to the Roundhouse on the site of the World's Fair. It was cleaned and restored and it has been there ever since. For British Columbia, it's the most significant existing piece of history.

I was telling this to Dave, who was clearly interested. "Go on," he kept saying. "I didn't know this."

"Didn't you go to school in BC?" I asked.

"Yes, that's why I didn't know any of this."

So I said we would do a story about the 374 and tell all this to the public. He was happy, because his seed of an idea was turning into a ripe fruit ready for picking.

He found a parking space right in front of the Roundhouse and we went inside—and the man with the beard wasn't there. There was only a woman in a wheelchair.

"Are you a volunteer?" I asked, trying to be friendly.

"Yes," she said, and told us her name was Cathy.

"Is there a man with a beard working here?"

"He's Ed and he's gone to the bathroom," she said.

"Thanks. We'll wait."

While we waited I looked at the locomotive and thought about the story it could tell. The same train, the same piece of black steel 125 years later. It was massive and hard and ready for the road again. It was beautiful. The story would be good.

Then Ed came back and we talked for a moment about the train. He knew the history of the mighty 374. He could tell it blindfolded at a rock concert. While we were talking, Cathy pushed the controls of her chair with her fingers, which don't bend, and drove it closer to us.

Ed didn't stop talking, but he saw something else that needed attention. He reached down and fixed Cathy's hair.

There are some things stronger than a railroad. A train is just something that crossed a country and held it together. A man touching a woman's hair that is caught in back of her wheelchair holds us all together.

Love beats steam engines any day. We did the news that night on the friendship of Cathy and Ed. The train could wait.

14

A Little Education

The phone rang. "Do you remember me? You called me Little Miss Sunshine?"

OMG. "Who?"

"Little Miss Sunshine. I did it. I did what you said. I graduated from UBC."

"Wonderful."

Who? There is no way I could forget anyone I called Miss Sunshine, even if she was little. Except I did forget. I am lucky, I meet many people. Most are unforgettable. I'm sure Little Miss Sunshine was, too, except I couldn't remember.

Put it together, Michael, and put it together quickly—she is still on the phone. UBC, big-time education, advanced studies, Sunshine.

Nothing.

"Remember, I got off the bus in front of the women's shelter and you called me Little Miss Sunshine."

Oooooh.

I remembered. A pleasant, slightly plump, smiling woman

who got off a bus at Jackson and East Hastings after I had been trying to do a story about a woman planting some flowers along- side an emergency drop-in shelter.

"Tell me about the flowers," I had asked.

What I got told instead was that I had to talk to the woman in charge and we should not take any pictures of the flowers.

I didn't mention that they are on a public street. I hate to enlarge on a problem even if someone else is presenting it.

The woman in charge sent out a second woman in charge. The lesson there is be wary of giving authority to anyone because it will surely go to the ego and inflate it.

The second woman in charge said they were being planted for a celebration and they would issue a press release about it in a few days and we could come back then. I mentioned they could get publicity for their event right now and it would help their event because, although I didn't mention it, their press release might wind up on the press release slush pile and be missed.

She said she'd been told to tell us there would be no comment.

I left, sad, because bureaucracy is a sin and it hurts those who use it.

I crossed the street and started reading a sign on an old apart- ment house on the corner. It said this was where Sadie Marks lived in 1919 when she met Benny Kubelsky. Sadie and Benny later changed their names to Mary Livingston and Jack Benny and went on to incredible fame in radio and television.

Right here? Right on this corner in this apartment house? Wow! That became a story on the news and was later in a book.

I had just turned around from the sign when a bus pulled up and an excited young woman got off.

She talked to me as though she knew me. Of course, there was a cameraman nearby and she had seen me on TV. That helps with the recognition factor.

"Hello," she said. Then she added a bouquet of nice things about the day and asked why we were there.

I told her about the shelter and the flowers and she said she was on her way to that same shelter and she agreed with me that sometimes people in charge of things let it go to their head. We talked just a little more and she told me about things she wanted to do with her life. Then she added she probably wouldn't be able to because there was no way for a woman like her.

What is a woman like her? Poor, uneducated, unemployed, unemployable, and a former drug addict. If I was at the track and her past performance was listed below her name, she would be a long shot, probably 100-1, the kind you don't bet on.

I had just finished writing the book about Reilly and about getting what you wanted if you really wanted it. I was probably talking about that too much, but I told her that she should go back to school. There are classes for everyone everywhere and many of them are free, I said.

She brightened up even more and I said she looked like Miss Sunshine. I added Little as a extra compliment.

But that was two years ago and now on the phone I only remembered the name Sunshine.

"This is Gladys, Miss Sunshine, and I've graduated from UBC."

Can't be, I thought. It hasn't been four years since the Jack Benny/Mary Livingston story and please don't tell me you got a degree in less time than I can write a book. I can't stand that.

"Not really a degree, but I passed one course and it was at UBC. Come to my school."

I arranged to meet her at her school a few days later. Her school is at the corner of East Hastings and Gore. It is in the First United Church, which has turned completely into a shelter and help facility for the homeless. There used to be church services inside. Now the homeless sleep there and are fed there, and in a corner room they are taught to read.

That was Miss Sunshine's school.

"Let's go in the side," she said. "The people in the front don't like cameras. They are either shy or trying to hide from someone."

This is not a school for the timid.

As we walked inside she said, "Education is the best thing in the world." Then up a few steps and she said, "I wish my sister could see me now, but she died last year."

"Sorry," I said. "From what?"

"Drugs. Too much drugs and the street. She had a hard life."

Miss Sunshine was sad when she said it, but she also said it in a way that was accepting. If you live by the code of the street you are not shocked when you hit the curb.

Then, instantly, quicker than a breath, she cheered up.

"Welcome to my school."

The door was open. Her face was beaming. Her voice was musical.

Behind us, passing by in the little hallway on their way to a free lunch, were those who were still living by the street. In front of us was a room with tables in a circle.

An immigrant from Africa named Augustine, who had wide, excited eyes, said hello.

"What do you think of Gladys?" I asked.

"She's wonderful. She's an inspiration."

Yesterday came in with an unhappy face. "That's her name," said Gladys, who wanted us to meet all her schoolmates.

"Why are you called Yesterday?" I asked the thin woman who had survived a long life in a few years.

"Because someone else is Tomorrow."

I couldn't argue with that. But there was Sunshine in the forecast.

"What do you think of Gladys?" I asked Yesterday.

Yesterday was renewed. "She graduated!" she said to me. "Did you know she GRADUATED!"

"That's why we are here," I said.

"Do you want to see it?" Gladys asked.

I already knew what she wanted to show us, because she was taking a paper out of a large brown envelope that had UBC written on the front.

"This is the most important thing of my life."

She took an official-looking paper out of the envelope and held it up. Her shoulders went back, her chin went up and her cheeks turned into dimples.

"When I get enough money I'm going to frame it," she said.

It was not a four-year degree. Not yet. It was a certificate for completing Humanities 101, a course in writing about your personal world. It was issued by the University of British Columbia.

"She worked so hard," said her teacher, Linda Rider.

Linda's main job is helping the students learn to read, or to count, although in truth a few were also working on computers. There is no telling what level anyone can climb to.

"Gladys wanted to learn," Linda said. "She wanted it desperately."

Linda helped her get enrolled in the UBC extension course. She pushed her, and Gladys did it. Gladys wrote all her assignments longhand in a notebook. She cannot type. The notebook is now filled with words and thoughts and observations.

I read some of them. There was no self-pity, no blaming, no complaining.

Then Gladys said to me that I deserved the credit.

I was lost. I had no idea why she said that.

"You told me I should go back to school," she said.

"But you did all the work. It is you who deserves the credit, you and your teacher and your dedication and . . ." By now I was fumbling for words and she interrupted me. It was on the video tape inside the camera.

"I wouldn't have done it if you hadn't told me to do it."

One passing remark. One note, not very original, just something you would say to anyone who was lost in life. You should go back to school.

"Honest. I would not have done it if you hadn't said it."

It was the right time, the right place, and the right feeling. It didn't need me—anyone could have said it. She could have seen an advertisement, perhaps on television, saying school is good. It was just a fluke that I said it. Anyone at any time can say to someone else something that can change everything. We should never miss the opportunity.

"No Gladys. Forget me. You did it. And you know it."

The 100-1 long shot came in first and was standing in the winner's circle. I wished there were flowers being put around her neck.

"That's my sister," she said, pointing to the top of a bookcase and a photo of a smiling woman who looked a lot like Gladys.

"She would have been so proud," said the new graduate.

And then she went back to work, writing in her notebook, and I went back to work wondering how to find words that could even come close to describing how warm and bright Miss Sunshine made the world.

15

Whistling Bernie

I have tried three times to write a novel about Bernie. It was to be happy and funny and tough and gritty. It was going to be full of broken rules and big successes, and music, always music coming from his whistling lips.

I just don't know how to write a novel. I don't know how to invent a fictional character that would come close to the real character.

Also I thought he was dead and I could finish the novel after I retired.

"Would you like to do a story on the Burnaby Library Talking Book program?" a nice lady asked me by email.

"No," I thought. Libraries have their own publicity departments and it might be dull watching someone listening to a tape recorder. Prejudice comes in many forms.

The next sentence in the email was, "I don't know if you know about him, but retired police sergeant Bernie Smith is one of our clients."

"What? He's alive? Yes, I want to do a story about him. When can I do it?"

I got to his home early. It was an ordinary old stucco house. Somehow I thought it would be bigger. I knocked on his door.

"Who's there?"

"McCardell from Global TV."

Response through the door: "Not here, you've got the wrong address."

I am gullible. There is no one else around. No library vehicles. No one delivering a stack of tapes or disks or whatever. I turn around and start to leave. I have the addresses in a notebook in my car.

The door opens. "If you are going down the steps I got you."

I turn around. There is Mr. Cool, wearing a smile accentuated by a white moustache over a black turtleneck and a small silver necklace bearing a tiny tail of a whale.

Bernie was eighty-eight and he could have been headed for a downtown club.

"I haven't heard anything about you for thirty years," I said.

"Thirty-two," he said. "Since I retired."

Before that Whistling Bernie Smith was the best-known policeman in the history of Vancouver. He insisted on walking one beat during most of his career and that was the toughest one, East Hastings. And his section of the street was the toughest part of East Hastings, between Main and Carrall.

If you had that "look" about you, something that might be suspicious, you could count on hearing the whistle catching up to you.

"What are you doing here, young man," he would say to the one with the "look."

"Nothing. What's it to you?" would say the very tough young man with the "look."

Bernie would smile and tilt his head. He knew the "look" and he knew how to face it with his own look. He wouldn't get angry.

"Would you accompany me over there for a moment, to that alley," Bernie would say.

"That's illegal. You can't make me and you can't beat me up. There are witnesses."

With barely a firm touch of his arm, the young man with the "look" would move to the alley and there Bernie would tell him things about how to avoid being hurt, either by him or by someone else on the street, someone with an even worse look. Bernie would give understandable advice, down-to-earth suggestions about living and where that living should take place, which was not on this street.

And then Bernie would send him on his way. In a few minutes you could hear Bernie whistling while he walked his beat.

I know because the young men and women to whom Bernie gave lessons usually didn't do anything wrong after that. I heard about his reputation before I started working down there and I learned it first-hand from working out of the press room of the police station for the last eight years of his career.

He was at the end of the old-time police method of walking the street and talking to the people on it and knowing who was there and what they were doing. It worked, and Bernie made an art form of it.

Then he retired, and disappeared. Actually he went fishing. It was decades later that I got that call from Janet Ritchey at the Burnaby Public Library.

Bernie suffers from macular degeneration. He cannot see. He feels for the phone and the door and his coffee cup and he shows me his whale tail necklace. "My daughter gave it to me."

But he still sees what is funny in any situation and he still whistles.

He does "Can you name this tune?" and he whistles well enough that most can.

His wife died a few years ago. They were married a very long time. But about those books:

When he had eyes that worked he used to read two books a year, maybe fewer. Now that he cannot see he goes through fifteen a month and they are delivered to his home. A box full of CDs arrives with several library workers and they tell him the titles and they talk about the books and Bernie chooses a stack.

He likes crime stories best, he told me.

Janet shook her head. "He likes soppy romances, too."

"Just once more, can you whistle a song for us?" I asked.

He put back his head and did the impossible. Okay, I want you to try to whistle on command. You can't. No one can.

Bernie did. It was classical. It was beautiful. I couldn't name the tune. Only Mozart could.

16

I've Got a Problem

It's April 27 and Howard has called, Howard White of Harbour Publishing, which publishes these books. He is an amazing guy, generous and patient. He lives way up the Sunshine Coast and is as laid-back as most of the people who live up there.

He called to say they are about to announce that I am going to have a new book. They are doing it on Friday. That's in two days. That's impossible. Already?

In the early years Howard supplemented his book business by driving a bulldozer. Then he gave a hungry ragtag army of local writers a chance to be read. He also had some big names. With my books he gives a great deal of the profits to the Variety Club of BC Children's Fund. Obviously, I like the guy.

However, I have fallen way behind on writing this book and there are deadlines. You can't just turn up with a book whenever you feel like it. That would be like a sock factory making no socks until they got into a sock-making mood. The world would be filled with toes sticking through holes in old socks. We need socks, we need books, and we need them on time, but I have not been pulling up my socks.

I have spent time gardening and a garden takes a lot of time. When I was a kid I woke up to concrete and went to bed with the same. The only thing we saw grow was the mould on the baloney.

And I've been spending time with my granddaughters. There is nothing else in the world as good as that. With one of them I built a dollhouse and read stories. With the other I chased her around in circles. Those things are important and they take time.

I have also spent a lot of time looking at the sky. That is one of my favourite duties. I look for holes in the clouds. If you have read the other books, you know that. If you can find a hole in the clouds you can get your message through and once you do that everything works—but it takes time to find the holes.

Right now I have 20,000 words. It needs 70,000. This is impossible. That means working day and night for ten weeks and I haven't actually worked for the last forty or so years, not since I found out that if you like what you are doing nothing is work. That's one of the secrets of life, but it's not really a secret. Anyone who is happy knows it. You just have to tell yourself that you love doing what you are doing and the work part of it disappears.

That applies to coal miners as well as artists. I met a couple of coal miners once and I thought they had the worst lives of anyone on earth. Their faces were black with soot and I know their lungs were the same.

"It's great down there," one said. "In our world we are in charge."

"We love the danger," said the other one. "Especially the respect we get when we come back up to the ground."

That was a strange set of words. They came back UP to the ground. Just the thought of that scared me. They have one of the meanest, hardest, dirtiest and most dangerous jobs on or under the earth, and they loved it. It wasn't work to them. You can feel good about anything.

Heck, writing a book in two and half months is nothing compared to that. In fact, you could do it. You should try it. Do what I do. Look at something neat and wonderful and happy or powerful or brave and write it down. If we were having a race we could both start now.

Write something now, something you have seen today, something honest and true and something that made you feel good, like meeting a couple of coal miners or whoever you meet, and when you are finished you will have a story and be on your way to a book and, most importantly, you will have a good night's sleep.

I can guarantee you'll have amazing dreams. Whenever I am writing something, anything, about something or someone, I have dreams that night that are better than going to the circus. The characters I've been writing about can suddenly fly and invite me to dinner and the meal is all vegetarian steaks with beer that doesn't make me ill or fat.

You know what dreams do, good dreams? They make you so happy you have to go back to sleep after you get up to go to the bathroom, just so you will have more dreams. If you write something about your day this will happen to you. I promise. Just try it.

You and I can have a race. You write every day, and in the fall—when and if this is published—you will see what I have written. You will look at your story and say, "Wait a minute, I'm better than that McCardell guy. My story is about someone I just met today and he/she is the most fabulous person ever and anywhere."

You get that feeling when you meet someone, talk to them and scribble something about them. I know because I do it every day and that's why my life has been a joy and my dreams are so good.

But it is so much better when you do it yourself. When you find someone or something that is wonderful or happy or touching or whatever, it's a real-life experience. It is yours, and it's better than reading about it or seeing it on TV.

So start tonight or tomorrow and find something. Write about it and talk about it and I'll go back through my favourite stories, and when we get to the end of this book we'll compare our stories. Your stories will be better—I know they will, because they'll be yours. This book will sit on a shelf and gather dust. Your stories will be with you forever.

Not a bad deal, right?

I know I have a head start because I've written 20,000 words and you haven't yet begun, but you can catch up. Give yourself six months or a year. Try it, get busy. Howard is waiting for you. I am waiting for you. And no one is going to be disappointed.

In the end you may send your stories to Howard and he may say, "Where have you been all my life? If only McCardell could learn to write like you."

Try it. It's better than watching television.

17

High Points of My Life

This is easy. Some of you know some of these stories, most of you don't. If you do, enjoy them again. There is new stuff in each of them. If you don't, stay tuned.

My father spent a lot of time in the bar on the corner of our street. Sometimes, when I was five or six years old, he would bring me there and I would listen to the men brag about how many Japanese they'd killed, although I know my father was on an island after it had been cleared of the enemy.

I would drink Cokes and draw circles in the water on the bar.

At home my parents would argue. This is nothing surprising for many families. My mother would hide my father's shoes and lock him in the bedroom to keep him home. He would climb out the window and walk down the street in his socks waving his fist at her.

It was a colourful life. This was before television, but who could ask for better drama.

We lived with my uncle, my father's brother, who was a New York City police detective. I don't think he liked his brother.

He would wear a suit every night going to work and I would watch him get dressed. He'd put one pistol in a holster strapped to his leg. He'd put a second pistol in a holster under his arm. He'd hook a black jack over his belt on the right side. He'd attach handcuffs to his belt on the left side. He'd put some extra bullets in a small packet in his side jacket pocket.

Then he'd give me a hug.

When my father came home much later my mother and I would push a dresser against the bedroom door while he hammered on the other side of it.

"Don't worry," she would tell me as we leaned against the dresser. "Your uncle will be home in the morning and everything will be okay."

Then my father would fall asleep outside the door.

In the morning he'd have gone into another room and my uncle would bring home detective friends of his. My mother would cook them breakfast and I would sit under the kitchen table listening to the stories of crime and rooftop chases and fights, and laughing.

I wanted to be a cop.

I asked him every day and he would say, "Some day, when you are old enough."

My mother would tell me not to bother him.

One day he came home with a bruised face and Band-Aids on his knuckles. My mother told me to leave him alone, but I didn't. I asked him if I could be a cop today.

He said, "Yes, today you are old enough."

He told me to raise my hand and promise to obey the law and protect my mother no matter what and he gave me a card with a picture of a police badge on it. I was a member of the New York City Police Department. I was six years old.

Then he went to bed.

I was a cop. I shoved my plastic six-shooter into my belt and tried to arrest people in the neighbourhood when I saw them stealing a neighbour's newspaper or dropping empty cigarette packs on the street or letting their dogs poop on the sidewalk.

The next morning I told my uncle that I had arrested all these people and told them that they had to come to him and he would take them to jail.

He put me on his knee and squeezed me very tight. My cheek went into the handle of his gun. He didn't get mad. He told me I had done very well, but arresting people came when I was a little older.

I knew I had done something wrong, but he didn't get mad at me. More than sixty years later I still remember that. When you don't get mad at someone it is more powerful than when you do.

He then asked me to teach him how to be a cowboy. I told him I would. I got my broom horse and my cowboy hat and the same plastic six-shooter and rode off, waiting for him to finish his breakfast so I could show him how to ride.

Time passed, as it does until you die. Then you don't know it. Before sunrise one morning my mother woke me up. She had a suitcase in her hand. She told me to put my coat over my pyjamas and come with her.

We left and took the subway across the city to her sister's apartment. I didn't see my father again for fifteen years. I never saw my uncle again. All I heard was that he retired early and moved away.

When I got out of the Air Force and was working for a big city New York newspaper I looked up my own name in their extensive files. That was like someone writing their name into Google now, just to see what would happen.

There was my uncle's name, and in the file there were photos taken secretly of him collecting payoffs, bribes, protection money from shopkeepers along a busy street.

He was a crooked cop.

I don't care. When I was little and needed him he was there and he didn't get angry when I did something wrong.

Some day, in the Cariboo, in cowboy country, I am going to rent a horse, maybe just inside a corral, and take my uncle's memory for a ride and teach him how to be a cowboy. He deserves it and he has waited a long time.

18

Cardboard Ocean

My mother and I lived in a row house next to the railroad tracks. That sounds very self-pitying. It isn't. Everyone I knew lived there.

The big passenger train went by close enough for me to almost read the newspapers in the hands of the passengers, if I'd been able to read. At the end of the street was another train, the infamous New York Elevated line, the El. It was noisy as 'ell. When it passed by, all talk on the street stopped. All instruction in school, which was on the other side of the tracks, stopped. And worst of all, you couldn't hear the radio, so when Superman was flying off to save the world we never knew if he actually did it.

As I mentioned earlier, and in my second book, *Back Alley Reporter*, we had very little money. There were no tennis courts or ice rinks or day camps or swimming pools. The nearest beach, the famous Coney Island, was two hours away by subway and none of us knew how to get there or had the money to ride it.

Our street was surrounded by factories. It was a very busy, very noisy neighbourhood. One of the factories made ice cream.

You can't wish for better than that—not because of the ice cream, but because they threw out tons of cardboard boxes and all of them were clean, unlike the other factories, whose cardboard was covered with grease.

The boxes weren't flattened, like good environmentalists must now do. They were tossed uncrushed into a fenced area against a wall of the factory. They were piled up two stories high, about six feet wide and more than twenty feet long.

That was our swimming pool, our ocean. We would climb the fence and get onto the roof of the factory, and then dive into the boxes. We could swim all day, under water without coming up for air.

Sometimes someone would find some broken chocolate wafers that were thrown out instead of being used for ice cream sandwiches. He would try to stuff them into his mouth before the others heard him chewing, but you can hear a lot of things under cardboard, even with traffic on the street. Kids' ears are designed to hear the crunch of chocolate wafers. We would swim down and chase the wafer thief, who had to pull his way through the boxes with his hands holding crackers, which wasn't easy.

Further below him were the little kids swimming and, like guppies, trying to catch the falling pieces of broken crackers.

This was our summer. That is, until the kids from another street tried to take over our ocean. There was no such thing as sharing. It was them or us and we fought with tooth and nail, meaning biting and scratching—even the girls. We couldn't give up our cardboard ocean.

Someone shouted, "STOP!" It was loud. It was strong. It was one of the workers in the freezer. He was Greek. They were all Greeks who worked in the freezers. They were the new immigrants and people complained that they were different from us and they talked differently and they were taking away jobs. Of course, none of *us*, or at least the *us* who complained, wanted to work in a freezer all day.

The Greek doing the yelling wore a big white parka. He had a giant moustache that covered most of his mouth, and he had an ice hook hung around his neck.

We had seen him watching us when he took his smoke breaks in the sun.

He could have spoken in any language and his meaning would have been clear. "No fighting," he said. "You race. The winner stays here. Loser goes away."

"We don't want to race," said one of the intruding kids. "You don't own this place. This is a free country."

The Greek stared down at the kid. "You race or I fix you so you don't race ever again."

We picked Joey because he was the strongest. He had a little brother who had cerebral palsy and couldn't walk, so Joey carried his brother everywhere. That was why he was strong.

They picked Rocco because *he* was strong—and ugly and mean. I added that last part because I always tell the truth.

The Greek stood at the edge of the roof overlooking the boxes and told Joey and Rocco to climb up. "You," he pointed at Rocco, "you climb that end. You," he pointed at Joey, "this end. When you get here you jump in and climb to the bottom and then come up. The first one at the top wins. His side stays."

They climbed the fence, the Greek said go and they dove into the boxes. We stood outside screaming and cheering. Rocco's gang kept spitting on the sidewalk. That was nasty and we wanted to fight again, but not now.

We couldn't see either of them because they were buried deep inside, but we could tell where they were by watching the boxes moving. Joey was fast, but it looked like Rocco was sliding down on grease. We had never seen anyone get to the bottom so fast.

The faster he went down the worse we felt.

"You're going to lose, ha, ha." That's what his gang was shouting. "Lose, lose, lose!"

We were praying.

Rocco was already starting up before Joey was at the bottom. And then something happened. Rocco started cursing. We didn't curse, at least not the words he was using. We weren't goody-goodies, but we weren't that bad.

We watched the boxes on Rocco's end get shoved around. We could tell he was climbing up, but then there were more bad words. The movement in the boxes was going down again.

Meanwhile, Joey had reached the bottom and was starting his climb back up. It wasn't easy. We had all done it. To climb straight up through a mountain of boxes was tough even for a wiry ten-year-old, but Joey was getting there, box by box, and we were cheering.

Rocco was cursing. We shouted to Joey, "Keep going." Rocco's friends shouted at us to shut up. There was some pushing and shoving outside the fence while inside Joey got higher and higher and Rocco cursed louder and louder.

Then at the top we saw Joey's arm come up and then his head. Rocco was still cursing. He crawled out through a hole in the fence just above the sidewalk. He was covered with chocolate syrup.

"No fair," he said. "It's a do-over. I couldn't climb. I kept slipping."

From the roof we heard the Greek shout down, "This side wins." He was holding Joey's arm up like a prize fighter.

Rocco's friends surrounded him, but they didn't want to touch him because he was a mess. His arms and shirt and hair and legs were dripping with dark chocolate.

"We got to do that again," he said. "This wasn't fair."

By then the Greek and Joey had come down the ladder inside the factory.

"You go," said the Greek to Rocco and his friends.

"No, it wasn't fair. I want another race. I want to get cleaned up and do it again, and I want Joey to go on this side."

"You go," said the Greek. "Go, get out of here."

"No," said Rocco.

The Greek took his ice hook off his neck and held the point in front of Rocco's face. "I said you go, and you don't come back."

Rocco and his friends left with Rocco dripping chocolate behind him. The Greek went back to work and we climbed up the fence and onto the roof.

We could see way down to the end of the block and we watched Rocco and his friends disappear into the shadows under the elevated tracks. We were so happy we could hardly talk. If we had lost this pile of cardboard it would have been a long, hot summer.

Then someone noticed that at the other end of the roof, where Rocco had gone down, there was an empty five-gallon can of chocolate syrup. We stared at each other. We all knew what had happened.

"The Greek fixed the race," someone said. "The Greek did it. He made us win."

We looked down on the sidewalk, which was empty now because he was back at work, and someone said, "Thank you, Mr. Greek."

I don't remember if we went swimming again that day or waited until the next day when they would clear out the boxes and start filling it up again. They did that at least twice a week so we always had fresh boxes to swim in.

We spent the rest of that summer swimming and talking about the Greek and sometimes, when he was having coffee and smoking, we would wave to him. He would smile back, or at least we thought it was a smile. It was hard to tell with his moustache.

We never knew why he did it. We didn't ask. We were afraid to ask. We just knew he did it and we thought Greeks were wonderful.

At the end of the summer the factory closed for the season, the Greeks were laid off and we went back to school.

"What did you do this summer?" a teacher asked some of us.

"Went swimming in Greece," one kid said.

"Of course you did," she said and shook her head. It was going to be another long year with imaginative little lying kids.

Luckily we didn't have to tell her we went to the beach or day camp or the neighbour's swimming pool. She would never have believed that either.

*   *   *

Eva Lonquist wrote to me a while ago saying she had read my earlier recollection of this story to her grade 8 class and they liked it. I wrote back and thanked her and said I was rewriting it for this book because it is one of the best days of my entire life and I didn't think very many people knew about it. That is, people outside of her class. She said she would be reading it to her class next year.

Then I told her there would be something new in the story this time.

That was a problem. There was nothing new. The story is now as the story happened then. Much more than half a century has passed and my memory of that day has the same images of the same boxes and the same race and the same chocolate.

Over the past few years I have had a strong urge to find some of those kids that swam in the boxes. I tried Facebook and Google. Nothing.

Then, after I had sent the manuscript to the publisher, I got an email from my cousin in New York. I have written about him before. When my mother left my father we moved in with her sister, who was my cousin's mother.

My cousin, Dick Reichert, was very happy about us moving in. He not only got moved out of his bedroom for us but out of the apartment. His bed and books went into a cubbyhole room at the top of the stairs outside the door to the world of his parents. This was like leaving home and being on his own, and he was only ten years old. His mother was not happy about this, but he was thrilled.

Later in life, when he went into the Air Force, I thought he was a hero. In the places where I have written about the Cold War and the bombers that took off around the clock from northern air bases in the US heading for Russia, he was one of the flight line mechanics who kept the airplanes flying. He watched the nuclear bombs getting loaded for each flight.

Anyway, in July I got an email from him that contained a newsletter from the Michelin Tire company, where he had once worked. It had a story about the passing of one of their long-time employees, Joe Colacioppo. It said he was a happy guy who was a good family man and had been a combat soldier in Vietnam, although he never wanted to talk about that.

My cousin said he met Joe more than a dozen years ago. He said he was a heavy-set guy who wore a motorcycle jacket and was very likeable. Joe had mentioned that he knew me. Coincidence.

When Eva Lonquist reads the story to her new class she can add one thing. Joe Colacioppo who passed away was Joey who won the race in the boxes. It is the same thing that happens to all of us, but when you know the person who died it gets inside you and for a few moments you remember the boxes and the day, and that person comes alive again.

19

Germany Taught Me Everything

I was so lucky. At fourteen I was a lost kid on the streets of New York. I didn't like school, I didn't understand anything in school and I liked wandering the streets, so I found a simple solution: Skip school and walk the streets. My mother was at work all day and she would never know.

You may know this story already, but the odds are against it. I wrote about it more than ten years ago, but these events had a greater effect on my life than just about anything else.

Back to school: Every few days I would find a postcard from the junior high school saying I was absent again. I would write on the back, "Mike was sick," and then I would sign my mother's name, or at least as close to her signature as I could copy. It looked like a largely illiterate attempt at forgery and it would never have fooled me, but I was only trying to get it past the teachers. Easy.

Then I mailed it back. Luckily I didn't even have to put a stamp on it. The board of education paid the postage both ways.

For four months I wandered about, learning a lot about the candy stores, the back alleys and the vagrants of the streets. At night, when she came home, my mother would send me to the corner to buy dinner. It was the same every night—four hot dogs, a half pound of potato salad and a tomato, "and make sure he gives you a good one."

I walked to the corner deli, right under the pounding elevated train, and bought dinner. "I vill give you the best tomato," the man always said.

Every once in a while, as he was working, his sleeve would go up and you could see the numbers tattooed on his forearm. His wife had the same. We all knew what it meant. He never talked about it, he just smiled. He always smiled and laughed, and he and his wife joked and talked almost without end.

And sometimes he would say to me as I left, "Don't vorry Mickie, dings vill get better. They alvays do."

He was an expert in that.

And then one night my mother got a call at home. They wanted her to come to school, and bring me.

"Did you sign all these cards, Mrs. McCardell?"

"What cards?"

My days of wandering were over, but then, a month later, things got better.

My mother came home one night and asked if I wanted to go to Germany.

All I knew was that they lost the war, and people were leaving Germany.

"When?"

"Next week."

Sometimes good things happen quickly. My mother worked for Radio Free Europe, one of the many organizations that were fighting communism during the long and scary Cold War.

She did nothing dramatic. She was a teletype operator, but a very good one. She could take dictation on a keyboard and she could type in almost any language without having a clue as to what she was typing. Both those qualities were important in an organization that had many secrets and dealt in many languages.

This is the part of the story I could tell a hundred times and it wouldn't be enough.

A week later we were in Munich in an apartment house with machine-gun bullet holes across the front wall. It was the only building left standing on the street. Every other building that wasn't entirely crushed was a shell. I walked by the fronts of them and looked in through the empty windows and saw the sky.

Most of the former apartment houses, though, were just piles of rubble. It had taken the Germans twelve years just to clear the bricks and wood from the street, and the only place to put it was back on the sites where the buildings had been.

At night the street was black. No street lights. Almost no car traffic. Almost no one walking. No noise.

During the day I saw many men going to work, most walking, many on crutches. I rarely saw a man with two arms and two legs. The ones with no legs pushed themselves around on boards with small wheels. They were only a few inches above the ground and used wooden sticks to move their broken bodies around.

War has its drawbacks.

I met two kids who became my closest friends. One was a boy named Alex. He had escaped with his mother and older brother from East Germany. They had walked at night carrying almost nothing. During the day they had hidden in fields and forests. He spoke English and Russian and German. He couldn't believe I didn't like school.

"That is the only way," he told me. He didn't explain to where. That was clear enough to him.

He taught me chess, we explored the bombed buildings

together and he told me about living under communism. Some of his stories were hard to listen to, even at the age of fourteen.

Not long after that I read the first book of my life—*Auntie Mame*, a comedy about a rich woman taking her nephew on a tour of Europe. My mother brought it home from work and I read it word by word, slowly. It was wonderful.

And then I went to school, and did my homework.

I also met Sonja, my first girlfriend. She had been in the Hungarian Revolution two years earlier. When she was twelve she stood in the street in Budapest and threw flaming bottles of gasoline at Russian tanks. I no longer thought I was such a tough kid.

The Cold War was the reason for Radio Free Europe. The Iron Curtain was the obstacle. The object was to send news over the curtain while the Russians did everything they could to jam the airwaves.

The Russians were adamant about this. It wasn't a game for children. The radio station had concrete barriers around it to stop trucks from backing up to it with bombs. Guards with sub-machine-guns walked up and down in front.

One day, inside the building, a spy or a double agent or whatever he was put cyanide in the salt shakers in the cafeteria that was used by all the employees. Another spy beat the information out of him just as the cafeteria opened in the morning. He ran screaming down the hallway and burst into the dining room yelling for everyone to stop. "Freeze. Don't move. Put down your forks."

The news was told to my mother, who was typing it on a direct link to headquarters in New York. She had eaten at home that morning. She said her fingers froze when she heard what had happened, and then she went on typing.

There were lessons to be learned in school and outside of it.

By the end of my first year in Germany I was German. It doesn't take a teenager long to adapt. Like all the boys I wore leather shorts. The good thing was they never needed washing and the more you wore them the more comfortable they became.

I also had an old bicycle and rode in and out of the city learning what bombs can do to churches as well as apartment houses, which didn't seem right. I also met a lot of German kids. It seemed like every other one was an orphan. I know the same thing happened in England. War is not good for families.

Then, one day, totally without planning, I rode for more than an hour outside the city on a road that was completely empty. There were no US Army jeeps or trucks, as there were on most of the other roads I had seen. There were no worn-out German delivery trucks filled with vegetables. There was no one walking on the road.

At the end of the road I saw why. I rode into Dachau.

The gate was broken. It was a huge gate. Above it was the infamous sign, "Arbeit Macht Frei." Work Brings Freedom. It did not.

This was more than ten years before it was cleaned up and made into a living museum of death. I was alone. I think the sky was grey. If it wasn't it should have been.

There were rows—row after row after row—of ovens out in the open. They were rectangular, and they were long. I don't know how long, but they were long. The openings, square at the bottom with a semicircular top, were about at my waist level.

I looked inside one of them. It was filled with ashes and bones. I leaned in, I don't know why, and I fell forward. My head and shoulders were inside. I put one of my hands out to catch myself and my arm went into ashes and bones up to my elbow.

This was thirteen years after the killing had stopped.

Outside the ovens were hills, everywhere. Hills that were knee high and hills that were waist high. They had weeds growing out of them, and pieces of bone between the weeds.

It was silent. The only sound was my shoes on the ground, which had ashes and bones everywhere. I walked and saw more ovens. Everyone had heard about this and I knew, everyone knew, the ovens were the only things here that were without pain, because by the time you got to the ovens you were dead. You had starved to death until your knees were bigger than your thighs. Or you'd been beaten to death. Or you'd been worked to death. Or you'd been experimented on in a laboratory without anaesthetics until your insides had died, slowly.

I knew all this. This is what the man in the deli who sold me my hot dogs and tomato didn't talk about. This is why he always said, "Don't worry, things will get better."

They had to, or they had to stop.

The door to the gas chamber was open, and I went inside. There were gouges in the walls from finger nails.

We had joked about this when I was younger. We said, after someone lost a ball game, that he would be sent to the showers. The showers were what the prisoners were told they were going to when they went to the gas chambers. It was a cruel joke. We knew what it meant but we didn't know what it meant. That is true in all things.

I left Dachau, walking away, pushing my bicycle. I didn't think. I didn't think that everything would be different because I had stood in the place of pain and humiliation and anger and hate and violence and unfairness and viciousness and death long after it had stopped. I didn't think it would change my life. I didn't think that at all.

But it did.

If you ever get the chance to help someone, do it.

If you ever get the desire to hurt someone, don't.

It is pretty easy to live if you know that.

20

The Day the President Was Killed

Many of the people I work with tell me they remember the day John Kennedy was assassinated. They were sent home from school by crying teachers. When they got home their mothers were crying.

I remember, too, but there were no tears. There was terror.

I was going to college in lower Manhattan, near where the World Trade Center would later be built. I was talking to someone out on the sidewalk when a fellow came running across the street screaming.

"The president's dead. The president's dead. He's been shot."

There are few shocks that are more profound than that. "Your mother is dead. She's been shot. Your child is dead. He's been shot."

JFK was family to most. The musical *Camelot*, with its rain only falling at night and everything being beautiful in the day, was the Kennedy story, or at least we all thought so.

He was young and handsome and brave. Jackie was young and beautiful and a new mother who had previously suffered a miscarriage. She was brave. She was remaking America as a place of beauty and grace and dignity.

He had faced down the Russians when they put missiles into Cuba. I was watching him on a ten-inch black and white television in an apartment in New York when he looked into the lens, into my eyes and the eyes of millions, and said he would not back down.

He told Nikita Khrushchev to remove the missiles, or else.

I went into the kitchen to tell my mother to come and listen. She was staring into a cup of tea. It was all going to end, soon. She didn't want to watch.

She had been born during World War I. She got married and had a child, me, during World War II. She left her husband during the Korean War. Her son, me, was in the Air Force during the Vietnam War. Her grandchildren were born during that war. She would never know that her first great-granddaughter would be born during the first Iraq War. Her second would be born during the war in Afghanistan.

She had had enough.

At the moment when she was saying no, that she would not watch the president, a wave of B-52 bombers was taking off from an air base in northern Montana. It was heading toward the North Pole and then over the top of the world to Russia. The planes carried city-destroying arsenals of nuclear bombs.

My cousin was in the Air Force then. He was a mechanic keeping those airplanes flying. We were very close.

From 1945 until the Soviet Union disintegrated in 1989, those bombers were always in the air. As soon as one wave of pilots neared the fail-safe line of the North Pole, another squadron took off, all loaded with nuclear bombs. The fail-safe line was the turnaround point. They had to get orders to turn back. If they didn't get the orders they would keep going.

For forty-four years there was never a minute when those airplanes were not in the air. That was part of the chill that was the Cold War.

At the same time, Russian airplanes were doing the same thing and Russian submarines loaded with missiles were sliding about the bottoms of the oceans trying to be in place when, not if but when, the orders came to fire.

Above the waters US Navy ships were hunting the subs. The Russians had more subs than the US. The US had more airplanes.

Both had many missiles sunk into silos across vast areas of the earth. I was once at an Air Force missile base in the northern part of the US. There was nothing there, nothing I could see. I had been at other air bases and there were airplanes, but not here. Here was just a vast emptiness, hiding countless silos, each with a missile. It is hard to think of it even now without shivering at what might have been.

My mother knew all this. Everyone knew this. There was no point in watching the president confront the Soviet premier. If he won, we could still lose. If he lost, well, it was only a matter of minutes.

Kennedy won. He didn't blink.

We loved Kennedy. And then he was killed.

My friend and I went into a bar. It was so crowded we pushed to get in. On a small television near the ceiling at the end of the bar Walter Cronkite took off his glasses, wiped his eyes, and said, "The president is dead."

There was not a sound in the bar.

I rode the subway uptown to the *New York Daily News*, where I was a copy boy. The riders in the subway stared straight ahead. No one was reading or talking or sleeping. Their eyes were blank.

I walked from Grand Central Station down 42nd Street. It

was always filled with horns and shouts and the noise of construction, but it was silent. Not one horn. The cranes had stopped. No talking. No running. No scooting around the person in front of you. Glassy-eyed people passed each other on the sidewalk but said nothing.

For three blocks there was silence. Cars stopped at red lights, then moved ahead when the light changed. There was no honking to push the car ahead to move.

I walked into the lobby of the *Daily News*. Always it was filled with tourists taking pictures of a giant turning globe sunk in a hole in the floor. There was no one there.

I rode the elevator to the seventh floor to the newsroom, then called the city room.

It was an explosion of people and shouting and typing and yelling and panic. They had called in everyone, everyone who could do anything. Reporters were supposed to have contacts with those who knew things; the Mafia, the courts, the police, the government, the church, the hot dog sellers. That was what they were paid for.

Every phone was being used. Every typewriter was getting hammered. I was grabbed by the shoulders and told to sit at the Foreign Desk and sort incoming teletype copy. Sort it into Kennedy stuff and other stuff. I had never sat at the Foreign Desk before. I had only delivered copy to it.

In minutes the floor started filling with crumpled paper, paper that was ripped out of typewriters when new information came in and made the last sentence being written inadequate.

In time, I couldn't judge how much, but in time, the crumpled paper covered the floor and was getting deeper. Much later I told people the paper was up to our knees. It wasn't, but it was over the tops of everyone's shoes.

The story of the assassination was number one. Everyone

knew that. But there was another story, a more important story, the one that was being written with terror.

Who could push the button?

Only the president had the code. The president had an army officer standing ten feet away at all times with an attaché case handcuffed to his arm. The world was constantly on the razor's edge of war. Only the president could push the button that would pull the trigger if the bad guy on the other side of the world drew first and started firing.

If the president was dead, who could fire back?

No one.

Somewhere deep underground in Moscow, generals and politicians were saying, "We have a ten- or fifteen-minute window when we can fire first and they won't shoot back. They will not respond. Let us do this now, or forever regret that we did not."

And some other Soviet generals and politicians were saying, "That is a stupid idea. We will just kill more of them than they kill of us, but we will all die."

They argued. The generals in America and Canada and England felt their blood pressure ready to blow the tops of their heads off.

In the newsroom of the *Daily News*, and in all newsrooms, the crumpled paper on the floor got higher. I kept sorting endless stories that were coming in faster than I could read where they were from.

We all knew there had to be a new president quickly, and it had to be announced quickly or there might not be a second edition of the paper, or the world.

In Texas, Air Force One was sitting on the runway with vice-president Lyndon Johnson. He was sworn in sixty-five minutes after Kennedy was killed. At his side was Mrs. Kennedy still wearing the dress heavily stained with the blood of her husband.

The official photographer had her turn her body so the blood wouldn't show so badly in the official swearing-in picture.

We didn't know. No one in the world outside of that airplane or an underground bunker under the Pentagon knew that the news of Kennedy's death had been withheld until the moment when the picture was taken. When Walter Cronkite read the official announcement of the end of one life, Lyndon Johnson had just been sworn in.

No one in Washington wanted anyone to know that there was no one in charge for an hour and five minutes.

More crumpled balls of paper were thrown on the paper already on the floor. The stories were jumbled and unverified and speculative and written and rewritten and checked and rechecked and the anthill of the newsroom was happening right before my eyes, whenever I could look up from the incoming stories.

The picture of the swearing in of Johnson went around the world as fast as the electric wires could move it. From that moment on, the nations ready to blow up each other were back to mutually assured destruction, which was the only thing keeping us all safe.

The stories kept coming and changing and I was at that desk from four in the afternoon until four in the morning when things started slowing down.

This is a note for the generation in high school that is not getting taught about the assassination in history lessons. You have to memorize the date, November 22, 1963, and then you will move on to another date and another assassination.

Raise your hand. Tell the teacher that was a terrifying day. Tell her or him how close the world came to almost not being. Then tell your classmates how exciting history is when you forget the dates and learn what the day was like.

21

Inside the Prison

There is another moment, an event, a "thing"—it is hard to tell what to call it—that shaped my life. It is mentioned in the flaps of all my books, and the story is in an earlier book, but there is more to it.

In 1970 the prisons inside New York were rioting. One after another went up in flames, literally, with fires inside while the prisoners were still inside and the firemen were unable to get in.

The fires were small (there isn't much that can burn inside a prison) but the smoke was thick and the chaos was blazing. Hostages were taken and threats were made and demands and negotiations went on.

Why did it happen? Easy. Prisons are not filled with happy, well-adjusted people who have much stake in life. The prisoners mainly got what they wanted in life by taking it, until they were caught.

We're not talking about the innocent ones who are wrongly convicted. That happens, and it is terrible, but most of the people locked away in small rooms have earned their place.

Then the prisons get overcrowded. It is hard enough to be in a crowded apartment that has a front door. It is unbearable when you cannot open the door. And then there is the sense of injustice felt by the people who didn't care about justice. Their food isn't good enough. Their exercise time is not enough. Their television time is restricted.

It's enough to make you riot.

One inner city prison after another erupted. That happened when news of one riot got to the next prison. Everything in life is contagious.

I was a young reporter with a young family. I was making just enough to pay for food and rent, so I was lucky, but there was no money left over for anything like a better apartment or vacations or savings. I was fairly typical.

On a Friday night I got paid. This was a different age. We got paid by cheque but could cash it right at the paymaster's window inside the newspaper office. I cashed mine and had my week's pay in my pocket.

"You should go and cover the prison tonight," I was told.

The rioting had been going on for several days and it was in a holding pattern now. Nothing new was happening and probably nothing new would happen overnight. The last of the politicians had finished trying to either make headlines for themselves or talk to the prisoners.

The politicians had spoken through the closed steel doors at the front of the prison.

My job was to be there in case anything happened and then to cover it as best I could while waiting for the big-name reporters to get there.

I sat on a curb reading a college book on psychology. I was going to school during the day. The curb hurt. The book was confusing. The light was bad.

A police sergeant came to me and a small group of reporters and said, "Any of you want to go inside? They want to talk to a reporter."

My arm shot up. "I want to go." It was better than psychology.

The photographer who was with me from the newspaper was older and wiser. "Are you sure?"

"Great opportunity," I said. "The story. We can get the real story."

I put my book down on the curb and asked a few people standing around to watch it. Then I thought of the money in my pocket. Whoops. I can't ask them to take care of it. I don't know them. I can't ask the cops. That would be even more foolish. They are all wearing the same clothes. They might be off shift before I got out. I might not get out.

I kept it in my pocket and we were brought across the street to the big, black, steel door. It was opened on the outside by guards who had the key.

"Go inside and wait," we were told.

We stepped into an entrance alcove about ten feet long. Bang. The door closed behind us. This was not exciting. This was not fun. We heard screaming and the banging of things on metal through the door.

"I am not happy about this," said the photographer.

The door opened and I was staring into Hell. Through the smoke a dozen faces stared at us, only I couldn't see their faces. They were wrapped in towels. I could only see the bloodshot eyes, all staring. Screams came from deep in the smoke behind them. Screams of pain.

And then the spears were pointed at our faces. They were wooden broom handles sharpened at the end and now pointed at my eyes.

"Don't talk. Don't do anything. Don't take any pictures. Follow us."

Someone said it. I didn't know which towel it came from. We followed and walked into a gut-wrenching stink of a mix of excrement and sweat. I had to breathe through my mouth.

We walked past cells with a few white prisoners still inside. They all had their front teeth punched out. They were used as sex slaves. We knew this. We had heard the stories. We could see it in their bruised faces still trying to hide behind the bars in the cells even though the doors were open.

We were led over catwalks three stories up between rows of cell blocks. We went back and forth from one side to the other. Had we been pushed over we would have been killed. We walked past hundreds of men, some with bare faces, looking at us like we were aliens. We were from the outside world.

We had the spears always inches from our faces. They were held by the prisoners walking backwards while in front of us. I could feel more of them behind us.

We walked and without moving my head I saw anger and hate and violence and desperation and ugliness and fear, enough to last many lifetimes.

This doesn't make them better, I thought. This doesn't punish them. They have their own world here the same as they have it on the outside. It is filled with the same violence and pain.

We were taken to the end of a cell block and there were four men, prison guards, sitting on the floor. Their hands were tied behind them. We were told to interview them and show to the outside that they were still alive. We could take a picture of them, just them, no one near them.

I talked to them. They all said they were being treated well. They all said they sent their love to their families. And then the interviews were over.

The spears were pointed back at our faces and we were walked back past the cells and through the smoke and past the staring eyes. We were held for several hours at the end of a cell block where faces with towels told us about the inhuman conditions in the prison.

And then, suddenly, we were brought to a small back door and it was opened and we were pushed out into the cold morning. A few policemen were outside.

"What happened?"

We told them. Then we left. A few hours later the picture of the four prison guards was on the front page of the morning paper and my story about what you have just read was the main story in the paper.

But I was home by then, trying to sleep for an hour before going to school and my psychology class. I told my wife about what happened. She knew nothing because there were no cell phones, no means of instant everywhere communication.

"And here is my pay," I said, pulling my hand and the cash out of my pocket.

Hundreds of violent criminals and no one had searched us.

*   *   *

That was not the story that changed how I saw things.

Two nights later I was on the roof of a warehouse across the street from the prison yard. I had watched hundreds of prison guards arriving during the night. They all wore heavy coats and many of them had football helmets. Many of them had baseball bats. The police armed others with nightsticks made of hickory and filled with lead.

From the roof I watched the guards go in through a back door to the prison. You couldn't see the door from the street.

I couldn't see anything else, but I knew what was happening.

The fighting that went on inside was horrendous. The guards

were rescuing their friends. They had righteousness on their side. The prisoners had nothing but their pent-up viciousness and their spears. What's more, most of them hadn't eaten for a week.

It was almost an hour later that I watched the guards come out, dragging the prisoners behind them. It is impossible to win against righteousness and nightsticks. About twenty guards formed two lines and forced the prisoners to crawl between them while they beat them.

They beat them savagely. They beat them without let-up or hesitation. They beat them if they stopped crawling. They beat them if they kept crawling.

At the end of the line the guards threw the limp, semi-conscious bodies onto a pile that kept growing. There was a lot of anger in that prison yard. If someone hurts your friends, generally you want to hurt them back.

I went downstairs and around to the front of the prison where the mayor was holding a press conference.

"The guards have taken control of the cell blocks and there has been no retaliation," he said.

From the back I shouted, "That's not true."

The cameras and microphones turned to me. I told them what I had seen.

The official version was confronted.

Back in the newsroom the old editors were skeptical. Had I actually seen what I said I had seen? Was I exaggerating? Could they trust a long-haired twenty-six-year-old reporter?

Over and over they asked how many had I seen, how many times did they hit the prisoners, could I see any faces? And most of all, did I really see what I said I saw?

The bell on the photo desk rang. Something important was coming in over the wires. One of the editors came back with pictures taken by an Associated Press photographer who was watching the same scene as me one floor below me. I didn't know he was there.

The editor dropped one photo after another on a desk. Each showed the guards hammering away on the prisoners who were lying helpless or curled up on the ground.

Then came a scene out of a Hollywood movie. The most senior of all the editors, a stern, unflinching man who had spent his life trying to make sure stories were true, looked at me and said, "Write your story, kid."

I couldn't blame the guards for doing what they did—I might have done the same—but it taught me one important thing: Don't ever believe the official version of anything. Period. The real victim of press releases is often the truth.

After that I took the subway to the bottom of Manhattan and went to school. Back to the psychology class again and everyone wanted to talk about the psychology of prisoners and retaliation and revenge, but the teacher said those things couldn't be discussed until there was a proper study of it. She went back to the lesson plan and, unshaven and smelling of cigarettes and coffee, I drifted off to sleep. Sometimes school was not a place to get an education.

The next day the *New York Times* wrote about me and my story on page one and later in the week I was credited in the *New Yorker* magazine for defying the mayor and shining light onto a lie. A grand jury indicted seven guards based on my story and the photographs.

Now, why am I telling you all this? Because when I watch a little girl taking her first ride on a scooter with her father running alongside her I know how good life can be, how truly good it can be.

You can believe that. Just be careful of the press releases.

22

Stop the Presses

"**W**e have a scoop," I said over the cell phone. "Stop the presses. The balloon was saved."

"The what was saved? The boy?"

The street was noisy. No wonder the editor in the newsroom couldn't hear.

I had said "Stop the presses" only once before. It was after two sons of a mobster boss had been shot. I was accidentally nearby and I got the story minutes after the first cop arrived and said to me, "Do you know who those guys are?"

He said it in a way that would make me fairly dumb not to know, so I said, "Yes, of course I know."

"Good," he said. "Then I don't have to explain."

Then he left.

I was only in the neighbourhood to get a pizza, it was one in the morning and I heard gunfire. I carried my pizza to the corner to see who was there, but I didn't go around the corner in case there was more shooting, which would have been a very bad sound to eat pizza with.

The shooting had stopped and what sounded like a hundred sirens had replaced it. Whomever it was I'd said I knew, whom I didn't know, must be important. In the early 1970s in New York an ordinary shooting got only an ordinary number of sirens. This was big time.

I went around the corner and saw a white Cadillac. Just getting out of it were two large fellows and two women. The men seemed to be protecting the women, hunching over them while they almost ran to a house about twenty steps away.

"That's Colombo's kids, you know," said another policeman, who was as young as me. He had just arrived and was obviously thrilled that he was at a big-time mobster shooting.

Colombo, I thought. Colombo? The only Colombo in New York who didn't go by another name was Joe Colombo, the head of one of the major crime families that was continually fighting with the other families. Families do that.

If they had just stuck with crime they would probably have done very well, but each family was greedy and begrudged seeing the profits of crime going to the other families and so they took the simplest action they knew—they tried to kill the other families. Again, families are like that.

At that time in New York there were seven major crime families, all Italian, all called the mafia by the public and the Cosa Nostra by the mafia. Cosa Nostra means "Our Thing," which is kind of a hippie phrase—"We're doing our thing"—except that when the mafia did their thing someone else always got poorer and then got hurt.

The same thing is now happening in Vancouver with drug gangs, which have their own fancy names: Red Dragons and Hells Angels. They don't look on each other as families, but they do the killing in the same way.

Back in New York, someone had shot at the sons of Joe

Colombo. Page one news. I was there long enough to learn the sons did not want to talk to the police, they had no idea why they were being shot at and they were legitimate businessmen with a family-loving father.

But they had been shot at, and by a sniper who'd been waiting for them, I learned. The gang wars had another incident.

I got into a phone booth and called the city desk while I was still eating my pizza. The truth is I didn't say stop the presses. I would never say that. I was too young. I told the city editor what happened and I heard in the background, when he moved the phone away from his face, "Stop the presses. Big one coming."

Then, with the phone close to my lips and a hope in my heart that I had enough coins (because every five minutes I had to put in another nickel), I told a rewrite man what had happened. He took another sip of beer, put a cigar in his mouth and started typing. I told him the story. This was one of those 100 percent my stories, so I got the byline.

In the composing room, which I have written about many times, the linotype operators were typing out, line by line, the copy from the rewrite man's manual typewriter.

Next to each linotype machine was a zinc ingot getting lowered by a chain into a glowing hot pot of the liquid type metal. Below the pot was an ever-burning flame fed by natural gas. The operators turned the ink on the paper copy into metal.

Then a printer took the lines of type and put them into a metal frame and in a few minutes all my spoken words that had become typed words came together again as metal words. Then an impression of the metal type was made on special cardboard, the back side of the cardboard was bent so that it was now curved, and it was filled with more melted metal. When the cardboard was removed, there was a curved, hard metal plate with the story written on it.

Then they stopped the presses and put on the new plate, a press man pushed a button and the presses started up again with the story about the gunmen who missed the sons of Joe Colombo on the front page.

Wow!

What happened in the days of competitive front-page news in newspapers was so exciting I couldn't believe it then and I still can't. Without satellites or cell phones or 24-hour news we got stories out within minutes of them happening. How could you beat that?

Answer: With a balloon.

This was just as exciting as hearing shots while eating my pizza. The blue balloon was bouncing down Georgia Street and then, whoomph, it bounced off the bumper of a bus. Whoosh, it was side-swiped by a car. It didn't explode. It didn't die. A balloon doesn't have a life, except when it has air in it, like the rest of us.

It doesn't have a life in the religious sense, except when it is battling to stay alive with nothing but luck on its side. It doesn't know it is trying to live, but I know it and everyone on Georgia Street who stopped to watch it knew that.

"I hope it lives," said a young woman.

"Why? It's just a balloon," I said, trying to be an antagonist and trying to hurry because the balloon was still going down the street and I had stopped to talk to someone because I *needed* comments about it but I didn't want to lose sight of it.

If you want to be a reporter or simply do good in life, ask short questions and don't hang around for long answers. Long answers let the subject get away, whether it is a balloon or the meaning of life. On the other hand, you do need input, you do need the comments of others, because no way in all the world are your thoughts alone worth listening to. That may hurt, but you and me, we're not that important.

And then it hit the windshield of a pickup truck and went up over the cab and the long box behind it. It was still alive. It had survived, so far. Please, let us get enough pictures of it so we can put it on television and, secretly, please help it.

Who was I asking?

Who cares?

"Do you care what happens to it?" I asked a couple.

"Of course; only a mean person would not," said a girl.

Maybe that's why I think girls are a higher form of evolution than boys.

Then it bounced to the sidewalk in front of a building near Thurlow Street and I saw one of two women reach out for it and it stayed there, as if it wanted to land in her arms.

I ran across the street. Okay, I'm guilty. I jay-ran. I went against the light. I was lucky the drivers were kind.

I didn't even think of where the cameraman was. I saw by his pictures later that he was still on the other side of Georgia. It is hard to run with a camera on your shoulder and one eye implanted in a scope.

The pictures were from a long way away and through traffic and showed me trying to stop two women.

"Excuse me. Please. Stop. Hello."

But they didn't hear me or they didn't think I was talking to them or they didn't understand me. Whatever the case, they kept going with the balloon.

I caught up to them and stopped them, which was met with some apprehension.

They were Asian. "Do you speak English?"

They were afraid. It isn't hard to see that someone is stepping back as you try to talk to them.

"Little."

"That's enough."

They didn't want to answer. They got that question all day in the classroom. But now someone with a microphone and no one else around was stopping them and they were smart enough to know that stepping backward was the wise thing to do.

The cameraman made it across the street, and suddenly they were two girls who were here to learn English who had become the target of a camera and an old guy.

"You caught the balloon," I said.

The woman with the balloon started to hand it to me. She must have been thinking that in Canada there are laws against snagging a wayward balloon.

"No, it's yours," I said.

She looked a tiny bit relieved, but still worried. One minute a blue balloon falls into their hands and the next they are being interrogated.

I tried to explain the television angle but that was useless. When you are talking about balloons don't switch the subject to things that are not balloons.

"Where are you from, where are you going, who are you?"

I get the questions out before anyone has a chance to answer, because I will take any response.

"We are from Korea," one of them said.

"Good, tell us in Korean what it means to find a balloon flying down the street?"

They haven't had this question in their ESL class. They didn't have this question in Korea.

"We wanted to save it," said one, struggling for the words, "because it was lost."

They might have learned that just an hour ago in class, one of those idioms that you drop in a foreign country. "I am lost. Here is my balloon."

Anyway, we won their confidence because we said their

English was very good. Then they said they had a friend whose birthday was this very day and they were going to see him and would bring the balloon for a present.

Knock me over with a balloon. The perfect ending for a lost bubble of air.

I called the office. "Stop the presses. The balloon was saved."

"No, not the boy, the balloon." Then I added, "Is there a missing boy?"

Answer from the other end: "No missing boy."

"Good," I said. "I have the balloon that was missing, but now it is found."

Short question from the other end, "Are you missing your mind?"

"No, but it's better to tell everyone about a saved balloon than an almost dead son of a mobster."

"What are you talking about?" the editor asked.

I held my cell phone close. "Look, once I wanted to say 'Stop the presses' for the shooting of a mobster's sons who didn't get shot, and that time I didn't actually say 'Stop the presses,' but I'll explain that some other time."

"We don't have presses," he said.

"I know that," I said. "But I wanted to make it sound dramatic."

"Is a balloon dramatic?"

"When it's saved it is."

"How am I going to write the intro?" he asked. The editor writes what the anchor reads before the story. He continued, "How about 'This is not about the shooting of the sons of a mobster whom no one in Vancouver knows about, but about a balloon, which makes no sense at all, except Mikey says it does.'?"

He meant it facetiously as a bad joke.

"Perfect," I said.

Now, in honesty, I was very excited when I was young and learning about the sniper attack on the sons of the head of a Cosa Nostra family, but it was much more fun and more exciting watching a balloon bouncing down Georgia Street and then getting saved and becoming a birthday present.

Nothing good happened with the shooting.

Something good happened with the balloon.

Good wins. No contest.

23

Carmela and Luppo

I t started with a sweet Italian lady and her little dog and ended with the eternal truth. We are all looking for that. Once you get it you don't have to learn anything else.

The story: Carmela was running down to the water to grab her little dog Luppo, who was going into the water. It was at Deer Lake Park. Please go there. It is so beautiful, it's in the middle of Burnaby and on an average day a hundred people will enjoy it and most of them live just down the street. It is near the Burnaby Village Museum, which will thrill you and your kids. It is as Burnaby was 150 years ago.

I doubt whether, 150 years ago, anyone cared if their big old hound went into the lake—it would just help get rid of the fleas—but times change and Carmela was chasing Luppo, again. Carmela was a woman who should have been full of the frustration of running after a dog that was going into the water again, and again, but that wasn't the case at all. As she explained to me, between frantic dashes to the lakeside, she suffered a great deal of physical pain and other problems too—except when she was chasing Luppo.

Luppo was a small white dog with long hair and a long snout who was in dog heaven when he was running toward the water. He spent a lot of time in dog heaven.

"Sorry, I can't talk to you, I have to catch Luppo," said Carmela.

That is all the interview we got from Carmela as she ran to the water to capture her dog, who was already waist deep (dog measurements) in the lake.

Carmela grabbed him and started wringing out the fur that hung dripping and soggy between Luppo's legs.

"I don't know what to do with him. He just loves the water," she said.

"Have you thought of a leash?" I asked.

"Oh, no. Then he wouldn't have freedom."

All I could see was that she wouldn't have to chase him if he had a leash.

But then I realized I was using the wrong word. If she had a leash she COULDN'T chase him.

Chasing him was everything she wanted, no matter what she said.

You get what you want. You always get what you want. That's what Reilly taught me.

Who's Reilly? You haven't read the last two books? No. Don't tell me that.

You know who Reilly is. You are nodding. Reilly changed my life, and if you've read those books I bet a quarter he changed yours, even if you only tried the Reilly method a little bit.

We have a fellowship, you who read these books and me. You know how I think, and why I think that way. I have explained Reilly's method to every reader of these books, to every cameraman, every editor, to everyone I know. I am not a preacher. I am not an evangelist. This is simply something that works and makes living a wonderful experience.

You get what you want. That is what Reilly, an autistic nine-year-old, told me. You always get what you want, if you believe you will get it, or if you believe you will do it, or become it, or achieve it or earn it. Whatever!

Do you want a couple of absolutely basic examples? Of course. Who would pass up brief but eternally impossible examples?

You are a man and you are old. Your prostate has enlarged. Many aging prostates do that. You are not a woman, because you have a prostate, but a similar problem arises with women because of reasons that are womanly and therefore mysterious.

You have frequent trips to the bathroom. Period. Salvation depends on Depends.

With a man it is because the prostate is next to the bladder and squeezes it. Can you imagine a balloon full of air, and then your fingers squeezing the stretched, taut rubber skin? If it's *your* bladder, you don't have to imagine it.

With women something else is going on, but again, anything to do with women is a mystery.

There are so many supplements for sale you could run out of time listening to their ads before you put down your cash and then hoped it would work. And if you believe it works, it might.

Or you could relax.

"Relax? I can't relax. I have to go to the bathroom. Are you crazy? I am using all my strength not to wet my pants and you say relax. You, sir, are a nutcase."

Maybe, but it works.

For years I fought it. I squeezed it. I literally squeezed it. I crossed my legs. I prayed. I was desperate.

Then, at one moment of crisis, which, as you know, happens

five or six times a day, I got distracted. I had work to do. The wind was blowing, the baby was crying, I forget which. I had to attend to the wind, or the baby.

Twenty minutes later I remembered I hadn't gone. Oh, brother, then I had to go, but what happened during those twenty minutes? Amazingly, I didn't have to go. I had no pressure, no pain, no crisis. That is impossible.

So try it, I said to me. The next time I have to go, think of something else and believe that it works. Impossible, I said. I'll have to go. I won't be able to think of anything else. I'll have to go. Thinking of something else is stupid and impossible and CRAZY. I'm selling myself a bottle of snake oil, whatever that is.

But it worked. Relax. Don't fight it. And it isn't in the not fighting it but in the believing that not fighting it works. Believe that if you are thinking of something else and relaxing, you won't have to go. Try it.

RELAX? If I relax I will have an embarrassing accident and it will be your fault, McCardell, and I will sue you for my wet pants and my loss of social standing.

Relax. Think of something else. Believe it will work. Believe in relaxing.

Try it again.

This is not a get-rich-quick scheme. This is not a path to heaven. This is not a way of improving your sex life, your job or your family's well-being. It is simply a way of avoiding a little wet problem.

It works—if you believe. Believe me.

Let's go over those instructions again. Believe you can do it. End of instructions.

Here's another example: Sneezing.

Are you crazy, McCardell? This is not a medical manual and

this chapter began with a nice story about a dog named Luppo and a woman named Carmela. How did it get into bladders and noses?

Easy. Carmela got what she wanted. You will see that in a moment. And as far as sneezing goes, do you have hay fever? Is your springtime a time of heck and darn? Does your nose have a feather jammed up one of the nostrils? Are your eyes bloodshot and watery without the benefit of alcohol? Is your life miserable?

Well, step right up and get the medicine. You could try the antihistamines, especially the ones that are non-drowsy and put you to sleep while you are driving home with your nose now dry but your eyes closed tight.

Or you could try, wait for it, you know it is coming, "I will not sneeze. I will not have a tickle in my nose."

"OMG, it tickles. Haaachooo!" Right into your sleeve, yuck because it was wet.

And then, again, more of the above.

"I can't stop. I sneeze and sneeze and I am weak and I am running out of Kleenex. And I am dying and I wish I was dead because I can't see, my eyes are so puffy."

Okay, we all have our problems. But try, I will not sneeze, I will not . . . haaachoo.

Try again. I am not kidding. I believe I will . . . haaaaaachh-hooooooo. I believe I will not sneeze.

Try again. It will work. You can control your life and your nose. And the tickle. You can. I know. Believe me.

Try again. It is better than running out of tissues.

Back to Luppo.

Carmela had carried him back to the parking lot and put him down when, bang, as if the starter's gun had silently gone off, Luppo shot off for the water.

"No, Luppo, no." Carmela groaned loudly and repeatedly.

He was running toward the water again. Carmela ran after him, but he made it to the water and went in.

"No," shouted Carmela.

She didn't want to go into the water with her shoes, but Luppo didn't want to go too far. It was as though they had both measured how far and how deep and had come up with the perfect compromise.

She reached out into the lake with only the toes of her shoes getting wet, picked him up and started wringing.

"You naughty dog," she said.

"Luppo, don't go into the water."

Then she put him down and he ran back in.

"Luppo. Don't."

He did. She picked him up and wrung him out.

She did this every day.

She walked back to the parking lot and told us how much he loves the water. She also told us he was the first dog in her life, and that she hadn't known how much fun he would be.

We talked about a leash again. She shook her head. Clearly what she really wanted was Luppo to go into the lake so she could run down, pick him up, wring out his fur, scold him and say, "Luppo, don't." She wanted to do this so it would seem like it was unplanned. Then she could go home and say, "You know what that crazy Luppo did? He ran into the water six times and I had to get him out every time."

It would be crazy if she wanted him to do it.

What does Luppo have to do with bladders and sneezes? Carmela was free of all pain and all problems when she was chasing Luppo. Her mind was on Luppo while she was pulling him out of the water and wringing his fur.

She forgot everything else. She didn't have to tell herself she believed she didn't have pain and problems: Luppo and the lake did that for her. She was living a different life. She was above and removed from herself. She got what she wanted, with a little help from Luppo and the lake.

You have pain and pressure and tickles? Focus your mind somewhere or on someone or something else. Chasing Luppo, for example.

You don't have a Luppo? Yes, you do. Luppo is the weeds in your garden that can never be conquered. Luppo is the book you never get around to reading. Luppo is the neighbour who needs some help.

Bladder pressure? Forgetaboutit. At least until you remember it.

Sneezing? "Darn. I'm going to...haaaaachooo. Wait. I haven't done that for ten whole minutes. How did that happen?"

You might call it the Luppo method.

24

Pike Place Fish

If you have never been to Pike Place Market in Seattle, you should go. Don't hesitate. Don't put it off. Go.

It is Granville Island with an endless comedy act. Yes, I like Granville Island. It offers much more than Pike Place. It has theatres and schools and a concrete factory and parks and a brewery and mini ferries and turtles in a pond and a duck crossing.

The Duck Crossing on Granville Island is wonderful. That is a touch of soul, but it is only a sign. Just after you pass the brewery and Kid's Market you see the Duck Crossing sign.

"Are you kidding?" I asked a maintenance man on the island.

"No way. It is serious. Ducks cross here. Drive carefully." He brushed off the sign with his sleeve. That is humour, but done quietly.

But in Pike Place Market there is a fish market, called Pike Place Fish Market. Brilliant original name. What goes on there has become world famous.

Half the workers at the store stand out in front of the boxes of ice and fish and crabs. They wear yellow rain slickers.

They wait for an order.

"A king salmon," says a customer. Customer points to it. King is American for chinook, which we think is the king of salmon even without the name.

One of the outside workers picks it up from the stacks of fish on ice, and then shouts, "One king." All the workers out front and behind the counter shout together, "One king." It is a powerful shout.

Then the outside worker throws it over the boxes and over the counter behind the boxes, a good twenty feet of throwing, where a behind-the-counter worker snags it. The fish isn't gently lobbed like in slow-pitch softball. The fish is thrown almost hardball style.

The crowd cheers.

The king gets weighed and wrapped, and then the behind-the-counter monger shouts, "King coming back."

All the workers shout together: "King coming back."

The wrapped six-pound fish flies over the counter into the hands of the receiver in the yellow slicker on the floor, who gives it to the customer and takes the money.

The crowd cheers and takes pictures.

"Two crabs, please."

A customer has spoken. The outside worker picks up the two chosen hard-shelled bodies and yells, "Two crabs."

All ten or twelve fish mongers yell, "Two crabs." The crabs, one at a time, fly through the air.

The crowd cheers and takes more pictures. The crabs get weighed and wrapped and, "Crabs coming back," is yelled.

More cheering. More pictures.

This goes on all day, every day. It may sound monotonous, but it works. The workers either really enjoy it or are paid to enjoy it. It doesn't matter. It is fun to watch. And the store doesn't have to advertise. Everyone who knows about it comes to buy a fish or wait for someone else to buy.

Souvenir stores in the market have cartoons and towels with pictures of the crowds of people watching fish flying through the air. All the cartoons show people clapping and cheering and taking pictures.

And then I saw the problem. It was the fault of the media.

A woman told me she had come from Boise, Idaho, and wanted to see the flying fish. She squeezed her way to the front of the crowd. She had to, she wanted a picture.

A man had come from Vancouver. He got to the front. Another woman from California and a man from Texas joined them. I know they were from California and Texas because they told each other loud enough for me to hear. They asked the man from Vancouver where he was from. With the lady from Boise they formed a solid front.

Then more photogs squeezed through the crowd. A bus must have unloaded just to watch the flying fish of Pike Place. "You can't miss this moment," I imagine the tour guide said.

In a few moments there was a wall of digital cameras and cell-phone lenses and expensive single-lens reflexes and little pink cameras and blue cameras and things I didn't think were cameras at all, all lined up in front of the counter, waiting.

"When are you going to throw a fish?" asked the Boise woman.

"When someone buys one," said the monger with the yellow slicker.

"I haven't got all day," said Boise lady. "I have to get back to my group. Can't you just throw one and let me get a picture?"

The monger in yellow knew the lady from Boise didn't catch the concept.

"Buy and fly," he said.

"But I don't want a fish. What am I going to do with a fish? I'm on a tour," said the Boise lady.

Yellow picked up a fish. More than twenty cameras rose up.

"I don't mean to be impolite, but all of you are in the way of the people who want to shop."

Then he put down the fish. Twenty groans and the cameras lowered.

I have seen something similar at almost every choir sing and gingerbread house contest I have been to in the last two decades. The cameras are close to the subject and in front of the audience. It is embarrassing. The poor folks who have come to see the event see only the backsides of the cameramen.

It is true that many more people will see the event on television, but I always think the cameras have long lenses. They could go at the back. The trouble is, you can get a better picture in the front, just like at the fish market.

There were no shouts, no fish, no pictures.

"Darn," said the Boise lady. "I have to go. It's not fair."

Yellow pants looked sad. "Wait," he said.

He picked up a king. "One king for Boise."

"ONE KING FOR BOISE," shouted all the fish folks.

It flew over the ice and the counter and was caught in mid-flight by two strong hands.

"I missed it," shouted Boise. "I wasn't ready. I didn't get it."

Yellow pants laughed.

"No, I think now you do get it. Hold up your camera."

He waited. "Ready?"

She said yes.

He held up his hands and barely glanced back.

"Boise fish coming back," the man behind the counter shouted.

"Boise fish coming back," all the workers shouted.

And the fish landed right in outside man's hands.

"You got it?" he said to the lady.

She was so happy she could only smile. At least nineteen other tourists also got the picture. They left and business returned to shouts and flying fish.

Moral? They know it in the fish store. If you want to get rid of a problem, treat it nicely.

That High-Flying Leaf

Hold onto your hat, or your heart. This is a shocker. Americans are looking up to Canadians for their patriotism. And not just love of country, but outward display of it.

No way. Impossible. Can't be. When I moved to Canada it was Americans who covered the sky with their flags. They were at rock concerts. They were at swap meets. They were on shoulder patches. Basically every police department in the country had a flag sewn on their uniform.

Yesterday, May 21, 2011, I was at something in Seattle called Street Fair. It is ten blocks of arts and crafts and food and music and jugglers in the university district and it has been going on for forty-five years. I hardly noticed at first, but there wasn't one American flag.

It used to be a Canadianism to say, "We aren't like Americans. We don't show our patriotism outwardly. We carry it inside."

That is very nice to hear, but I look out the window where I am sitting now in my home and there is a Canadian flag flying on

147

a pole in front of the house across the street, and it is very nice to see.

When I drive around the city I see the Maple Leaf flying basically everywhere. When I travel I see it sewn onto nearly every backpack and stickered on countless suitcases.

Some say it is so those carrying it don't get mistaken for Americans. Some Americans have said the same thing when they put the Maple Leaf on their American Tourister luggage.

Then in Seattle I read a story in an arts and entertainment newspaper headlined, "Fear of the Flag." It's in rock and roll and arts papers that you get a feeling of what the mood is in a city. Feelings inside tell you what is behind the facts that are outside and, more importantly, they can almost predict what the future facts will be.

Chris Kornelis, a music critic whom I don't know and have never met, said he had a good feeling when he was at a rock show in Pemberton three years ago. He wrote that after the warm-up bands played, "the crush of young, almost entirely Canadian, fans in front of the stage burst into an impromptu a cappella rendition of their national anthem, 'O Canada.'"

At an outdoor rock concert in Washington, Kornelis wrote, Canadian fans flew Canadian flags. One young American woman who lives in Canada but was back visiting the US wrapped herself in the red and white flag. He talked to her.

"I love America," she said. "My mom's American. But Americans don't share the same enthusiasm about patriotism as Canadians."

My eyes bulged. I thought it was the other way around. But no, right there in black and white and read all over, the newspaper fellow was saying, "It's commonplace to see Canadians make their national pride known at summer festivals... Such outward expression of national pride is unheard of among their stateside peers."

He said it is "embarrassing" for a young music fan in America to hold up the flag. The connotation that it "represents hicks, rednecks, the NASCAR community, and the far right is so prevalent that it almost doesn't make sense for a liberal to wave the flag anymore." That is the feeling in a newspaper, the *Seattle Weekly*, that has stories on music and the arts and feelings and trends.

In Canada he talked to someone who said the flag flies with the rock music because, "Every time we're having fun, we're patriotic."

As I said, the world has turned upside down. Or maybe it is right side up.

I think the Stars and Stripes is a proud and strong symbol and represents a long list of good things. But I'm glad to look out my window and see the Maple Leaf.

26

This Incredible City

Every time I look at Vancouver I get shivers. This is one amazing city that is so new, so old, so tough, so tender and sooooo fascinating.

The first thing you may be thinking is that I came from New York and how can I compare? Easily. NYC is a giant of history and excitement and culture and past crime and current peace. No fooling around. You go there and you feel it. The people who live there serve the city, which is a living organism.

Yes, I love New York.

But luckily I came here and, yes, I love Vancouver. The difference is that this city is the servant of the people. This city hasn't gotten so big and famous that it has overtaken life. You can still grow here and change the city if you like.

New York takes a movement to change it. Vancouver can be altered and can grow and improve by the work of a single person. If you dig away the garbage and plant a garden on a street in New York, no one except the locals will notice. If you dig up part of a back lane in Vancouver and plant flowers and zucchini you will end up on the six o'clock news, probably as the last story, and others will start doing the same thing and the city will grow and smile and it will be all because of you.

Not bad for a place of a million people.

I should tell you how I got here. This story is in an earlier book but the odds are you don't know about it. Judging by the number of sales of the book and the number of people living here this will be a new story. If you already know it, forgive me and just think, you are ahead of all those who don't know, at least for the next minute or so. Plus you will get some new information now.

After I got out of the Air Force in 1969 I went back to New York with my wife and son and daughter and returned to reporting for the *New York Daily News*. There was only one story, the same one every day: Crime.

The headlines over my byline were "Hostage Safe, Robber Killed In Escape Try," and "Woman, 3 Kids Wounded in 'Insane' Sniping," and "Deaf-Mute, 12, Defies Bully, Dies," and "Walks Dog, Gets Bullet In Head," and "4 Held For Murder In Shootout."

Young reporters always save their stories. I still have those yellowing pieces of newspaper. Now I save pictures of the flowers in my garden.

You get the image. New York then was just at the dawn of the crack epidemic that would bring the city to its knees. No, lower than that. It would almost kill the city. Officially the wave of crack and crime broke over the city ten years later. What I was seeing was the childhood stage, which was already unbearable. I've already told you about the time I was inside a rioting prison. All the stories that I lived through added up to New York not being a good place to raise children.

One day, while I was out at work, my wife was with our kids in a concrete playground when a gunfight broke out between the cops and the bad guys. They were shooting over her head as she lay on the ground with our kids under her body. There was no trauma counselling. It was just another day in the city.

Her father had a gun put to his head. My mother was robbed on the street and thrown to the ground. There were more things that happened, but the short of it is I was reading an article about Vancouver in *National Geographic* one day and it looked nice and I asked my wife to read it and then I asked, "Do you want to move there?"

That was all there was to it. We had no idea where it was, but it looked nice and the story said nothing about crime or drugs.

By mail I got a job at the *Vancouver Sun* and got the working permit to enter Canada, but New Yorkers really have no idea of geography outside of New York.

I rented a U-Haul truck for three days. I knew Vancouver was west of Montreal. I figured one day north to Montreal, one day west to Vancouver, find an apartment, unload the truck and the next day return it. The motor was running when an uncle of my wife's came to say goodbye. He handed me a map, one of those automobile association maps that fold out like an accordion. I started unfolding it. I handed one end to my son who was sitting next to me. He handed it to his sister who passed it to her mother who was next to her. I was still holding the other end.

"Where are we going?" I asked.

"There," pointed the uncle. "Hope you have a full gas tank."

I still have the receipt for the three-day rental. The rest of the trip was an adventure. You don't get rides like that at Disneyland.

Thirty-eight years later, my wife and I and our daughter are still here, now with grandchildren. Our son moved back to New York in time to watch it transform itself into a relatively crime-free city.

Sadly, crime has risen in Vancouver. I have written about why and what can be done in other books. In brief, crime is up here because of drugs, predominantly crack cocaine, from which there is unbelievable profit to be made.

By the way, if you didn't know, crack is called crack because when you heat a mixture of cocaine and baking soda to form crystals it makes a cracking sound. The crystals, which are like little rocks (for which reason they are called rocks), are then smoked, usually in a piece of plastic tubing, and the effect is like having a rocket ship take off in your head.

Those who smoke it, or who dilute it and inject it, say they would kill their mothers to get the money to buy it. It is obviously not good in the hands of the human species.

The situation can be changed, it can be fixed. Those selling it have to be punished in a way that outweighs the profits, and those taking it have to be weaned off it, whether they want to or not. That violates all manner of rules and laws, but if something is wrong you fix it.

Despite that, the one bottom line is I love Vancouver. And almost as much as I love this city, I love the really fascinating story of how it came into being. Don't think of this as history, but see it as a child who grew up in the wilderness and then walked out of the woods as a distinguished, tough, artistic, business-savvy adult.

27

The Family Album

In the beginning Greenpeace would have been happy. There were no golf courses, no landfills, just trees—and the trees were giants. They were twenty stories high, maybe thirty, and they were so thick that if you looked down from a cloud you would think they were mounds of gargantuan moss covering the land.

A few thousand Natives lived here and, aside from attacks from other Natives from the north in which they occasionally killed large numbers of the locals, everyone was happy. They ate oysters and salmon and deer and some of those mandatory vegetables so that they would meet the Native's Daily Requirements of vitamins and they were super healthy.

No obesity, no diabetes, no overcrowded emergency wards or clinics with doctors who have no idea who you are.

Then came Whitey. At first Whitey was nice. Whitey gave the Natives Hudson's Bay blankets, which were itchy, and guns, which were dangerous, and whiskey, like the first drug dealers, and they brought new names for old places, such as English Bay and Spanish Banks and Burrard Inlet.

"What's wrong with our names?" the Natives asked.

"Too hard to pronounce," said Whitey. "And besides, we have to name places after the people who paid us to discover you so they get the credit and will keep paying us."

"But we don't need discovering," the Natives said.

"How else can we civilize you and bring you into the world of stock markets and mortgage defaults and industrial pollution?"

"You have a point," said the Native chief, "but I think the point just stuck me."

In the next page of the album, Whitey cut down the trees. From here to there and back again. Everywhere. Chop, chop, etc. The axe was swinging and the trees were falling.

"We've got to cut them to sell them," said Edward Stamp. He was just up from San Francisco trying to make a killing in gold but that was too hard so he thought he would cash in on trees.

"Let's clear the trees out of this spot and make a sawmill," he said. The trees fell and thus was created Brockton Oval, although he didn't call it that. He called it his sawmill, saying this was the perfect spot for it. He would float the felled trees in on the water and slice them up on the land.

The reason he picked that spot was that he'd found a large freshwater lake nearby. It had beaver in it so he called it Beaver Lake. Next he ran pipes from the lake to his sawmill, which needed fresh water for the steam engines. Then he killed the beavers. He didn't want them chewing through the pipes.

The trouble was, Edward Stamp missed one little quirk of nature. If you go to Brockton Oval today and look out at the water you will see it flows one way and then, when the tide changes a few hours later, it flows the other way. Well of course! It is near a narrows, for heaven's sake. Edward, didn't you look? Sometimes, when the tide is very high or very low, it not only flows—it becomes a riptide, meaning it flows rip-roaringly fast. That happens a couple of times a month. If you float cut trees into that water you'll just curse as they shoot out to sea.

Just because you build a sawmill or run a business or think you are going to make a fortune doesn't mean your head is screwed on straight.

Mr. Stamp stomped his foot and said to his mill workers, "This is dumb. Let's move."

That is the only thing that saved Stanley Park. On the other hand, were it not for Edward Stamp there would be no cricket games played where his mill once stood.

There is a plaque on the ground near the seawall with Edward Stamp's name and a mention of his intentions.

If you would like to see how it looked before the trees were turned into everything except trees, go to West Vancouver. Some people say that city has never changed, but it has. At one end they built the country's first shopping mall and heading toward the other end of town they commissioned a mural of how it looked before the mall. In fact, before everything.

Just off Marine Drive at 25th Street, in the village of Dundarave, is a large painting of what the Lower Mainland looked like when Captain Cook sailed into town. Captain Cook was a cool guy. Fifty years before the British Navy figured out what was slowly and painfully killing its sailors he had the idea that they could be saved with something good to eat. So he gave them sauerkraut and limes. Brilliant. He knew nothing about vitamin C—no one knew anything about it—but he saw his sailors getting sick on every trip. They would start out healthy and then fade away and die.

Maybe he should feed them something besides rotten pork and leather-hard bread.

For reasons not known, he gave them pickled cabbages and limes. It must have come to him in a dream or a wild dinner party.

Either that or he liked pickled cabbage and limes and wanted to share.

The result: they lived, and they were able-bodied sailors from the first to the last day. My gosh. This was one of the greatest discoveries in the history of the planet. Half a century later the government and the admirals said let's try that. That was two generations of dying sailors later.

Why does it take people who are in charge of us so long to see what those of us who are their underlings figure out on our own? Governments are sometimes so slow it is heartbreaking.

Back to West Vancouver, where you can look at this mural for yourself and marvel about what happened when the pasty-looking white folks arrived and said, "You know what we can do with trees? We can sell them and get piles of money." This was better than gold because you had to find the gold. You didn't have to hunt for the trees. Don't worry about ecology. It hasn't been invented yet.

And don't worry about running out of trees. It will never happen.

Of course, we might run out of people to cut down the trees. You want the job? You can start right now, today, because you are replacing the last man who had the job who got flattened and killed yesterday when a tree fell on him.

The life expectancy in the woods was about six months. Workers' compensation hadn't been invented yet.

The giant trees were floated in to Burrard, further east, to the second mill that Edward Stamp set up. This one had no riptide at its back door.

It eventually became known as the Hastings Sawmill. The mill was massive. The lumber it cut was just as massive. The workers joked that they shipped out "Vancouver toothpicks." They were solid pieces of cedar three feet by three feet by sixty feet. Basically, they cut off the bark and squared the length of the trees.

The mill stretched between what became Carrall and Heatley Streets. To put it simply, the mill became the Downtown Eastside. If there had not been a riptide at Mr. Stamp's first mill, Stanley Park would have become the Downtown Westside, with bars and cheap hotels.

Besides making some men (it's always men) very rich, the most significant thing that happened at the mill was that drinking was forbidden. This wasn't to save the men, but to make sure they wouldn't harm the machinery.

Still, you know what happens when you tell someone they can't drink. They get thirsty. So a bankrupt British sailor named Jack opened a saloon, about one hundred steps outside the boundary of the mill. Brilliant. It was open twenty-four hours a day. He got rich. Soon there were other saloons and seven breweries pumping out beer. There was only one soft drink factory.

That first saloon run by Jack, who was called Gassy because he was filled with hot air (their way of saying he was always talking), was the embryo that grew into Vancouver.

Now finger-thin saplings are planted along the sidewalks of the city with tags on them saying, "Please water me." Give them a couple of centuries and they may take over again.

28

And the Name?

How did Vancouver get the name Vancouver? It would have been called Mud Flats if geography had anything to do with it. Or Clear Cut. We live in the great city of Clear Cut.

But no. In the beginning it was called Gas Town by everyone who lived in a shack close enough to Gassy Jack's saloon to drink his beer before going off to saw up logs or cut down trees.

Then it was called Granville after a British aristocrat who was the British Home Secretary in charge of the colonies. He was never in Vancouver.

At the same time, the fabulous Canadian Pacific Railway was ripping its way west, claiming large chunks of the land it was going through for its own. It was a private corporation uniting a country and putting much of it in its own pockets.

Today that would probably be illegal, but back then the railroad was heroic. If it came to British Columbia the people said they would join Canada. If it did not, they would offer themselves up to America.

The owners of the Canadian Pacific Railway thought this

would be terrible. The CPR was the Microsoft and Arabian oil cartels combined of its day. That is to say, the CPR owned everything that the Hudson's Bay Company did not.

The head of the CPR was an American, and rule number one when dealing with Americans is: Don't try to prevent an American from making money, especially from Canadian land by making it part of America.

"This land on the coast of the Pacific Ocean is Canadian," said Cornelius Van Horne, who was president of the Canadian Pacific Railway.

"And what land is Canadian can be served by the CPR. And what land is served by the CPR must be owned by the CPR."

You see, his business plan was simple. He sees it, he wants it, he puts down tracks to get to it and it is his. What bank would turn him down? Besides, he controlled most of the banks.

"We will build the railroad to the coast and the nice people of British Columbia will remain Canadian and then we can obtain the land that the railroad goes through for ourselves, meaning me."

In the history of this country that was a big moment. Otherwise we in British Columbia would now be buying our milk and gasoline for 20 percent less and we would be driving east to visit Canada.

All prevented, ironically, by an American.

But he couldn't stand the name of the town. He was sitting in a rowboat, being paddled around what would become Lost Lagoon, when he said, quote: "Who the heck knows about this Granville fellow? He's nothing." Well, I'm paraphrasing his words a bit.

"We have to call this great city, which the Canadian Pacific Railway owns most of (and I own much of the Canadian Pacific Railway), something grand."

If he were living now he would name it after Terry Fox, because he is greatly revered and everyone knows his name. Or Trevor Linden. Fox City. Linden City. Except they weren't born yet and the most famous person in the world at the time was Captain George Vancouver. He was like Neil Armstrong, the first man to step on the moon, except most Canadians or Americans have forgotten who he is.

Anyway, back then, everyone (everyone in the English-speaking world, and they didn't care about anyone else) knew Vancouver. He had at least sailed into Burrard Inlet and spent a couple of hours walking around. Van Horne said, "That's a good name."

There was no debate, no vote, no consultation or discussion. Van Horne said, while sitting in the back of a rowboat, Vancouver it will be—and Vancouver it was.

Luckily for us, Lady Gaga hadn't yet been born.

29

The Big Trench Story Again, with a Better Ending

It is engineering that makes you suck in your breath. It is imagination that blows your mind. At least my mind, because I pass by this every day and say, "They did what?"

I have told this story before because it is just so darn cool. I tell it again because it now has such a warm ending.

At the beginning of the 1900s Vancouver looked like it was on steroids. It was growing faster than a magic beanstalk.

Buildings sprouted. The population boomed. Real estate was hot. There was all the usual excitement and road closures that go with a growing city.

There were still trees to cut down and fish to catch and gold to be found. What more could you want?

A second railroad, of course. That is what we wanted. One railroad, like one car in your garage or one TV in your house, is never enough. "Pleeaase, dad. We only have one TV. That is so last century."

The city and the province had just one railroad coming to

town—the Canadian Pacific—and that had collected most of the best real estate in Vancouver, including the only good route into the city, the one along Burrard Inlet.

The Canadian Pacific Railway had done something wonderful. It had made British Columbians feel like they were Canadians and it had kept them from joining the US. On the other hand, the CPR owned virtually everything within a half-hour march of their tracks.

We want competition, said the people.

And we want some of the action, said the Great Northern Railway, which was desperate to get into this new booming town.

The only problem was, the only route left open for the Great Northern was under water, and steam engines don't do well under water.

What's more, before they got to the water the route into the city was uphill, and steam engines don't like hills.

So the railroad hired a lot of Chinese workers. This was before the White Canada Forever movement began smashing in the front windows of the Chinese shops to get rid of them. The railroad company gave the Chinese only one order: "Dig."

In a little over a year the diggers, with some steam shovels to help, dug a trench from Nanaimo Street and 12th Avenue to Clark Drive and 6th Avenue. It was a kilometre and a half long and four stories deep. That was a lot of digging, but it made the ground flat for the tracks.

However, at the end of the trench was False Creek, which splashed up against the hill of Clark Drive. How do you get rid of the water? Easy. They had all that dirt from the trench. Just dump it into the water until there is no water.

Splash. Down went the dirt, back went the water. More dirt, less water. Lots more dirt, lots less water. More and more dirt, until the original False Creek was a memory.

"Are you calling that False Creek?" said some old-timer in 1911. "That's a puddle compared to just last year. That was when False Creek was False Creek. It was a mighty little body of water. Now it's an embarrassment."

I've already told you about an actual old-timer living on 6th Avenue just west of Clark whose house was more than a hundred years old. He said that when it was built it was beachfront property. It is now a thousand yards from the nearest water.

The Great Northern Railway drove its trains through the trench and parked them on the land that used to be water and immediately did what many companies do when they spend all their money chasing an economic dream. They went bankrupt.

Penniless, the Great Northern Railway got its steam engines to the west coast and then couldn't afford to light their fires.

The young Canadian government politicians were understanding, or at least they understood the opportunity that suddenly appeared in front of them. They said, "We will take care of your problems. We will take over your railroad and eliminate your debt and give the railway to the Canadian people and we will call our new, ready-made train line The Canadian National Railway."

That's why you have CN today. You probably know that story.

And then came the new ending. After I did the False Creek story on television on the 125th anniversary of Vancouver, I got a letter. The first best thing about it was that it was handwritten. Many kids in elementary school now cannot write with a pen or pencil. I have heard this from their shocked parents. Their kids can type, with their thumbs, but not write with a pen.

The letter was neatly written. Doris Reese said the story on TV had brought tears to her eyes.

"Why?" she wrote. "I will tell you," she went on.

Doris could teach good writing.

Her father came to Vancouver in 1919 from Winnipeg to work on the CNR. They lived, as did most of the railroad workers, within walking distance of work in the Grandview area. She remembers the address: 1772 East 2nd Avenue. She was born there in February 1921.

When Doris was a child, her mother would bring her and her older brother to the Victoria Drive overpass to watch their father's train go by underneath as it started on its journey east.

"He would wave to us from the caboose as they passed below. I still have that vision very clearly."

When she was five years old her father was transferred to Kamloops. There they were "a very happy, very involved, young family for a few short years."

Short years? Why?

Doris should have written novels.

"My father (at age 40) and an engineer were both killed by a slide in the Fraser Canyon near Boston Bar on December 30, 1929. At the beginning of the Great Depression my mother was left a widow with two small children to support."

Her mother had no income or pension from the railroad, nor help from the government. I know that as a fact, but Doris didn't mention it. As with handwriting, she also learned pride and the strength not to complain.

She said she also remembers watching her brother come home from five years overseas during the war. He got off the train at the CNR station at Main and Terminal. It was the same station her father had walked into to go to work.

Doris wrote that her brother "marched through the doors back to us and, though he is now also gone, that station lives in my heart and will forever."

She signed her letter, (Miss) Doris E. Reese.

Doris, I thought the story of digging the trench and filling in half of False Creek was amazing, but your story is so much better. You made the first story come alive. Thank you.

30

The Good, the Ugly and the Amazing of History

This is not all a happy story, but it is amazing. This is not all a sad story, but it is unbelievable. Actually it is ridiculous and embarrassing and stimulating, but it really should be known.

This is HISTORY. OMG No! Please. I had it in school and hated it. They gave me a date and said this happened then, but the only date I wanted was with the girl two rows away who was so beautiful and who ignored me.

I failed history.

Well, heads up guys and gals. Guys and gals are historic words from a time when guys and gals went steady before they kissed. Now you kiss, then ask a name and sometimes a gender. Going Steady is a historic state of being that your grandparents did before they kissed, and then that's all they did—and you think you have it tough.

Heads up because real history is almost as good as Harry Potter. If you live in Vancouver, think of it as a person, and you are living inside one of the most fascinating living characters that ever walked this earth.

There was SEX. And there was GREED. And SEX. And DRUGS. And SEX. And the Ku Klux Klan.

What? The KKK was never here. This is Canada. We are pure. My friends are Chinese and Asian and West Indian. The Klan was in the US. The Klan was evil. The Klan was scary. But not in Canada, and certainly not in British Columbia and never, never in Vancouver.

Wrong, bucko.

Let me take you back to the HISTORY of a house.

Part one of the story starts with sex, as do many things.

A fellow named William Lamont Tait made a ton of money from lumber. That was back when there were trees. He had a home built in the new rich area called Shaughnessy Heights. (Don't worry. You don't have to remember any of this, but you will.)

William was from Scotland and the home he had built was super large and beautiful. It is on Matthews Street, just west of Granville, if you want to see it.

It has large domes with weathervane points on the tops, which look like part of a woman's body. Later it had the nick-name the Mae West House. She was a movie star with large round domes, with points.

Go look. You don't need the address. You will say the house looks like Lady Gaga lying on her back. The old lumber million-aires didn't do things by accident.

Tait called it Glen Brae, which is Scottish for a valley be-tween the mountains, which it certainly also looks like.

However, no matter what the owner called it, his neighbours hated it. No, it was worse than hating. They asked him to knock it down because it was embarrassing to their wives who had grown up under Queen Victoria's rule and knew that women looked different from men, but you don't mention anything about that in polite company and you never, never look at it.

This was the age when the legs of soft easy chairs in living rooms were covered with skirts.

So, tear down your house, Mr. Tait.

William Tait told them something about free speech or at least free expression, or maybe simply "Don't deny me my pleasures," or just "Go away." Of course, the possibility was there that no one understood him because of his accent. Anyway, he imported a high wrought iron fence from Scotland and put it up in front of his house. Battles with neighbours are nothing new and they happen on even the most exclusive streets.

The fence had rosettes in gold leaf as decorations and cost $10,000. You not only keep your neighbours out with your fence, but you can also use it to flaunt your wealth at them. The fence was more than ten years' salary for the average person hacking down trees.

The moral is you don't tell a rich man to remove the large round domes that bring him pleasure. "You can look at my domes," he was saying, "but don't touch."

There is no record of what his wife thought of it, but with eighteen rooms to wander through she may never have noticed the roof, or maybe she just said she knew what her husband liked.

On the third floor they had only one room, for dancing, and Tait had a thick layer of seaweed placed under the wood so that it would cushion the feet of the dancers. He may have done this for his wife, who had lost a leg and did her dancing on an artificial limb. He also had an elevator installed, one of the first in the province, so that she could get to the dance floor.

He was a nice, rich, don't mess with me, guy.

Then he got sick of his neighbours and moved into his own

apartment houses downtown so he could live where the action was. It is still there at the corner of Burrard and Robson. He called it the Manhattan, because for many people, then as now, that central part of New York is the centre of the universe.

Later Tait died. That happens.

Part two: Houses, like people, have many lives. In 1925 a group of vile men entered the front door of Glen Brae.

"Did anyone see you?" asked someone inside.

"No, we move by night."

Inside they gathered on the third floor and wrapped themselves with white sheets with loose sleeves and then put pointy white caps on their heads to fit their brains.

"We are the loyal Ku Klux Klan," they said together.

Actually they weren't satisfied with just being the KKK. They added two more Ks. They were the Kanadian Kouncil of the Ku Klux Klan. That was the KKKKK.

Just try saying five K's out loud quickly and make it menacing. You sound like you have a speech impediment and those you were trying to frighten would say, "You poor man. Let me recommend a therapist, if not for your head then your tongue."

They put on masks and went downstairs and paraded down Granville Street carrying crosses lit by electric lights powered by batteries.

"Be afraid, Chinese people, we are coming."

There were many white people in Vancouver then who feared the Chinese. The whites looked at the Chinese like Americans in the South looked at blacks. I hate you and I am terrified of you. Would you please just go away. And stop making eyes at my sister, even if she's looking at you.

The Canadian government had passed laws to keep new Chinese immigrants from landing here and the KKKKK and the white racists who preceded them did what they could to get rid of those who were already here.

They instigated mobs of whites to smash windows in Chinatown and Japantown. They got bullies to beat up Asians. They were not nice.

They also hired crooked lawyers to keep a ship full of Sikh immigrants from India from docking in Vancouver, even though those on the boat were British subjects and had the right to land here.

For two months they weren't given any fresh water or food. They returned to Calcutta where many of them were arrested and others were shot.

It would be so wonderful if the KKKKK would dress up to-day in their pointy hats and march through Surrey or Richmond.

"Wait, we were only kidding," they would shout as they ran, tripping over their robes.

This history has a part three, too. Many years later the house with the domes was given a different life. Children with cancer now go in through the front door. Their parents go with them.

The rooms are quiet, except when the soft laughter of a child is heard, and sometimes it's followed by the sobbing of a parent. They try not to cry. This is not a place to cry, not while there is life, but sometimes they can't help it.

The children, all of them, are so strong it defies belief. The children all know this is their last bed, in their last home, but few of them are afraid. Most of them tell their parents not to worry.

The children are five and six and seven years old. They know things the rest of us do not.

On Christmas Eve there are carols and a tree is decorated in the front yard where all the kids can see it through the windows. Some may not be there for Christmas morning.

The house is now called Canuck Place. The domes are still there but they are looked at differently now. Now they are a mother's breasts beneath which the children who are dying of cancer are sleeping.

The house that was shunned in the beginning and then carried evil is now more holy than all the churches and synagogues and mosques in the city. It is the children who give it a new life.

Go stand in front of it. The fence is still there. You can see the gold-leaf flowers. You can look back through the years and see the hooded evil men coming out the front door. You know the story. You can tell it and shock anyone who is with you.

But most importantly, you will feel the power of the lives of the children, the children who face death and are not afraid and who comfort their parents. That is a miracle. They erase the stain of the vile KKK. The children change everything.

Sometimes, on the road of history, we eventually find the right direction.

31

Bitter Tasting Sugar

Before we puff up our chests too much about how wonderful we are, it's good to know how bad we were.

We now have so many races and cultures living together it is basically impossible to go outside without seeing someone who is different from you, no matter who you are. In many families you can stay indoors and see the same thing. But let us go back to the very early days of Vancouver.

"How do we get rid of those slant-eyed devils," asked the city alderman.

"Why did we allow them in?" asked another.

"To build the railroads, you idiot, but we don't need them any longer. I wish they would just go away."

The reason for the meeting was not to get rid of the slant-eyed devils but to increase business in Vancouver, especially business for white folks.

First on the list of applicants was Benjamin Rogers. He was young. He was dashingly handsome. He was American. He had a proposal.

"I will build a sugar refinery in Vancouver," he said.

They liked this. This would be the first company not connected with selling off the forests or the fish.

Benjamin Rogers knew a lot about sugar. His father was the president of a sugar refinery in Louisiana. He also knew a lot about race relations.

Almost half the population of Louisiana was black. All of them had been slaves until that darn, inconvenient, war between the North and the South set them free just a few decades earlier.

His father knew that to keep the sugar coming he had to keep the workers working. The days were endless, the pay was miserable, and the conditions were like being slaves no matter what the colour of the workers.

So the workers did what workers had learned to do during the hard days. They went on strike.

Ben's father went out to tell them to go back to work or he would get new workers who would work for less. Someone threw a brick at him and hit him in the head and killed him. No more negotiations.

Ben left the South because he was not going to deal with workers who didn't like their jobs and killed his father. He went to New York and then Montreal and in both places he learned more about making sugar. He was twenty-six years old when he heard that Vancouver was close to the Philippines, from which sugar cane came.

Can you remember what you were doing at twenty-six?

He took a train across Canada and went straight to City Hall, where he offered to build a factory if the city fathers would give him a few special considerations.

One: He wanted $40,000 in cash. That would be like $4 million now. That was not to be a loan, it was to be a gift.

Two: No taxes for fifteen years. That would be sweet.

Three: Free water for ten years. You need water to refine sugar.

"Are you out of your mind?" the city fathers asked.

But young Benjamin knew what they were afraid of. He knew what he was afraid of, and he knew how to swing a deal.

"In return for this I will not hire any Chinese workers. Only white hands will touch my white sugar."

The city fathers rose as one: "Sign here," they said.

Rogers later had advertisements printed that said if you buy cheaper sugar from the Orient it will have been touched by yellow hands. Not many bought the cheaper sugar.

It is strange to think of that now when you're having coffee with a group of Chinese friends or if, in fact, you are Chinese, and you are putting Rogers sugar into your coffee.

Who is the one who chokes on that? You or Ben?

You are bigger than Ben. Besides, who uses white sugar now? Yuck. It is poison to good health.

But he wasn't evil. He was a man of his time. Coloured people were to be avoided and shunned and castigated. On the other hand, can you imagine having his business savvy when you were twenty-six?

Ben had also learned another lesson. His workers complained that it was unfair that the women employees had to stand for ten hours a day sewing up bags of sugar. They wanted seats so they could sit down. Ben said they could sew faster if they were standing, but when the workers walked out he remembered his father and left town.

Ben built his first mansion on Davie Street. It is still there, although it is boarded up right now. It is called the Mansion and it was Romano's Macaroni Grill for many years.

Judging by his sugar policy, Ben would have had the prevailing view of the men of that era, which would have included being staunchly opposed to homosexuals as well as Asians and blacks.

Little did he know that the street he built his home on would be renamed after Alexander Davie, a former Premier of BC who was the first openly gay politician in the province. When he died, his friends opened a community centre in his memory on the street that was now named Davie. Most of the men who came to the centre were gay. And then the street filled with friends of theirs.

Ben, I'm sorry to tell you, but your old home is in the homosexual capital of Western Canada and some of the customers of the restaurant that your home was turned into were gay, and some were Chinese and gay, and they ate in your old dining room.

32

The Chicken Shack

When you look at the stories of our past, it isn't only sugar that leaves a bitter aftertaste; it is also fried chicken.

The sumptuous, breaded, moist chicken came from Vie's Chicken Shack. One bite and your mouth was in heaven. Two bites and you never wanted to leave. Three bites and you thought you should get out of here before something happens.

What would happen? The police would raid the Chicken Shack? You would be caught in the raid and you would wind up in the newspapers with your name as one who frequented the world of the Darkies.

You couldn't live that down. The Darkies were near Main Street, all along Prior. They had music, something called jazz, and fried chicken and there were some women who would do what you wanted them to do if you paid them. Darkies did that.

Of course you might wind up killed and stuffed in a garbage can. That had happened, you know, at least once. That might happen in the white side of town, too, but over here you never know.

Hogan's Alley it was called, but it was more than an alley.

Part of the alley still exists, north of Prior Street between Jackson and Gore. The same kind of galvanized tin shacks that I saw in impoverished black towns in the Deep South are in that alley, but around the alley were homes. Music came from some of them, late at night, and in a couple of the homes that had been turned into homey restaurants you could get fried chicken, Southern fried chicken, the only place in Vancouver to buy it.

Some came from Vie's Chicken and Steak Shack a few steps east of Main Street. The smell was mouth-watering. It was the most famous restaurant on the East Side. Louis Armstrong and Nat King Cole ate there.

Nora Hendrix, Jimmy's grandmother, worked there, and Jimmy came up from Seattle with his parents to visit in the 1960s.

The all-white city fathers didn't like this black spot on their city. What would people think? It's bad enough we have East Indians and Chinese, but Negroes?

This was only thirty years after the formation of the White Canada Forever party, to which many prominent citizens belonged.

But how do you get rid of a neighbourhood? You can't pass laws against them. You can't just say please move, and Canadians are supposed to be civilized so you can't shoot them. This was a problem.

Solution? Brilliant. What Vancouver needs is a highway system criss-crossing the city. It could go north to south but let's start east to west.

We could extend Broadway or 1st Avenue or even Hastings Street. Those are all major thoroughfares. That would make sense.

But wait a minute. Look at this map. There is a tiny street called Prior. Almost no one uses it so it would be perfect to begin the new highway there. Oh, my gosh. It just happens to run right through Hogan's Alley. Who would have guessed?

So the residents were legally evicted and their homes were bulldozed and a highway system that runs exactly five blocks was ploughed through the sweet sounds of jazz and the mouth-watering smell of fried chicken. The only part of Vancouver that was exciting in the day and came alive at night was erased, forever.

You probably know the only part of the highway system that was completed. You hear it on traffic reports. It is the Georgia Viaduct. A few homeless people, none of them black, live under it now.

Right after it was finished, the city fathers changed their plans and cancelled any more highway building inside the city. And now, forty years later, the city fathers and mothers have said that the viaduct is ugly and doesn't speed up traffic and it should be torn down.

There is a tiny museum, the Jimmy Hendrix shrine, standing near where Vie's Chicken Shack once stood. The shrine was built by Vincent Fodera, who owns a youth hostel on the corner of Main and Prior. He was visiting the Jimmy Hendrix museum in Seattle when he saw that the address of his youth hostel was the same as the address of Vie's Chicken Shack.

There is some dispute over whether that is the exact spot of the Chicken Shack. It doesn't matter. The sound of Jimi Hendrix's guitar was heard on that corner. He is gone. The shack is gone. The neighbourhood is gone.

Only the story is left.

33

Island of the Dead

I was with cameraman Karl Cassleman who, as you know from previous stories, eats and loves life. He has a romance with everything around him and that makes him fascinating to be with.

We were talking about race relations and other heavy stuff as we approached Stanley Park. Heavy subjects sometimes come up. He said almost every race has taken other races as slaves.

I asked if he knew why Deadman's Island was called that.

He pretended to be distracted.

"Slaves were taken from this park," I said, because I love any excuse to make the point that basically anywhere you are is a time machine of hair-raising stories.

Long ago a fierce tribe from the north swooped down into what is now the park and grabbed up a bunch of sweet young ladies.

They were going to do what many early people did, and some current people sadly still do, and take them back home as slaves.

The fellows from whom they took them lived on the banks

of the park gathering oysters and catching fish most of their lives. The setting was so rich in food and so peaceful, it didn't produce battle-hardened inhabitants.

But they were good men. They didn't want their women to have lives of misery, so they got together and made a tough decision. A group of eighty of them walked through the forest, found the invaders and offered themselves up in exchange for the ladies.

The invaders had to weigh the benefits of this. They could become a conquering bunch of warriors who killed off an entire tribe of other warriors, even if the warriors didn't have weapons and didn't fight back, or they could be the ones who brought home the maidens who would do the cooking and cleaning and perform other duties.

Luckily for the ladies, and not so luckily for the men, the macho image won out. The northern invaders chose to kill the men. That would give them prestige, and when it comes right down to it, notches in your gun count for more than pots on the stove.

Not far from Siwash Rock the Stanley Park natives allowed themselves to be killed. They were all done in with sharpened spears made of tree branches. They all stood still while they were killed. They were doing it for their women. Their courage was beyond belief.

Then the invaders left. They had their reputation to spread.

Near what is now Third Beach, the women gathered together their dead lovers and carried them to an island on the other side of the park, which was not yet a park.

There is another version of this story. Every story, every history book, has many versions. In this version, the battle was fierce and 200 local natives were killed. Histories of wars are usually written by the victor. There is little mention of World War II in Japanese history books.

Whatever happened in Stanley Park, it was bloody. The women placed the bodies of their men in cedar boxes made by the few remaining old men in their families. Then, with ropes made of cedar bark, they hauled the boxes up into the trees. Up there in the branches they would be closer to the sky.

Can you imagine the pain of that day?

Karl and I had stopped near where the totem poles now attract the tourists.

Behind where a heron was standing in the low tide waiting for a fish was Deadman's Island. It is now a Navy Reserve Base.

"A hundred years later," I said to Karl, "a new immigrant named John Morton wanted to buy the island. He hired a rower in a small boat that brought him to it and he walked around and saw the boxes. He poked his cane into one and bones fell out. He called it Deadman's Island."

It then became a burial ground for the new white folks who'd moved into Vancouver, and during a smallpox epidemic in the late 1800s it became a quarantine site for victims of the horrid disease. When they died it became their burial site, under the ground.

Later someone wanted to build a sawmill on the island and they cut down all the trees. In World War I it was taken over by the Canadian government because it was strategic to the defence of the city. Now it is the HMS *Discovery*, the only ship in the Canadian Navy that doesn't float.

And while we were talking about that, we saw two of the huge horses pulling a wagon load of tourists around the park with Canucks flags tied to their halters.

A flag on a horse during the Stanley Cup playoffs is a current story that becomes history. Karl took pictures of them, and the woman holding the reins told us she was worried that someone would steal them from her car so she put them on the horses.

Then, as she left, we heard her telling the story of Deadman's Island to the tourists. And they thought they were just going to see some pretty scenery.

34

The Net Minders

I t was the third game of the San Jose series and they were not watching.

Whooah, stop the truck. "They're not watching."

"Who's not watching?"

"Whoever they are, they're not. That's good enough for me."

It is sometimes difficult to explain how stories come about. It is difficult enough for me to understand. Most days I am simply in amazement at the end.

"You mean we didn't know about this and now we have it and it's fascinating?" I say this to myself because how can I believe, for example, that I walk into the Roundhouse in Yaletown, as in an earlier story, to learn about the first steam engine to cross the country and end up with a tale of eternal friendship, no, truthfully, a story of love, between a man who looks like Santa Claus and a woman who has spent her life in a wheelchair?

How? Just luck, I guess.

No, it's belief that something will happen. You can do that same thing not just with stories but with everything in your life.

You can't do your homework, you want a promotion at work, you want to get along with your mate. All of those are impossible, right?

Wrong.

Believe you can and you will. It will happen, but you've got to believe it.

That is as well as I can explain it to myself, although it sounds very airy-fairy, so how do I explain it to a cameraman who hasn't seen the process?

His name is John Dowell. He has white hair. He is a production and sports cameraman, one of an army of shooters who keep shows on the air and industry growing. He holds a camera at the Canucks' games. He has a headset on for the whole game. He is close to the action. He is being prompted by a producer to get a tight shot, get a wide shot. It is non-stop action.

He has also just finished a video for the company putting the new roof on the stadium downtown. He has to be up there. He watches the ironworkers crawling around on the cables. It is not a job for the timid. He also takes pictures of gardens for horticultural publications. He has been doing this all his life, but everything he does is scripted. It is not news.

News is a different animal. News is trying to catch a ball when you don't know it's coming. News is not knowing what is going to happen and you still have to capture it even though it might not happen, or it happens around the corner.

News is having squirts of adrenalin for lunch and high blood pressure for dessert.

Unless, of course, you do it my way. Then it is simply a matter of believing and hoping and waiting and believing and searching and believing and luck.

"Where are we going?" John asked.

I crossed my wrists and pointed in opposite directions.

"Very good," I said. "You made a left turn. Now we're getting somewhere."

He is in news today because it is the Sunday of Victoria Day and there is a shortage of cameramen. I am working because I am in news. If you or your children go into news don't expect to be together at home for Sunday dinner, ever.

"The hockey game is on right now. Let's go by the stadium and you can show me what you took pictures of on the roof next door and maybe we'll see some kids playing street hockey on the sidewalk." I say all this knowing I can't see what he shot up there and there are no kids playing outside because it is a construction zone, but any start is better than complaining that you don't know where to start.

There are no kids playing and I cannot, of course, get on the roof.

We go by the Roundhouse. He asks about the steam engine inside. He knows nothing about it. I am happy to tell him about the engine that kept him from being an American. (You've already read this in the story of Santa and Cathy earlier in this book.) He says he is a product of the Canadian school system.

I say everyone in the city is inside watching the game so let's go to Granville Island where there will be some non-hockey fans shopping. Or at least I hope they will be.

Just as we are approaching the island I say, "No. Let's go to the fishing docks."

"Why?"

"It's good to change your mind," I say.

Remember, this is a man who works in a world where every shot is programmed and set up ahead of time.

"Maybe we'll find a fisherman listening to the radio on his boat," I said. But I know that won't happen because if they are not fishing and not fixing their boats they are not on their boats—these are not pleasure craft—and when the fishermen aren't working they are home watching the game in HDTV.

We drive slowly by the open lockers where gear is stored and that is where the, "Whooah, stop the truck. They're not watching," came.

A round, strong, burly man was mending his net. I know "round" and "strong" together mean "burly," but he was more than just round and strong. He was burly on top of that.

For fifty-nine years Mack West has been fishing.

"You're not watching the game," I said.

"No, I want them to win. When I don't watch they win."

Bingo. Perfect. The goal light went on. What more could I hope for? See, from nothing came this. Not bad, I am gloating inside myself.

"He's twitching to watch," said a native woman ten steps away mending the same net. "But he doesn't want to jinx them."

"Does he like hockey?" I ask.

She demonstrates how he dodges and weaves while watching. "He's got a stick, he's the goalie. He shoots, he's the centre. He scores," she said, and she laughed.

John is taping her talking. I see he is smiling. Who would not smile at discovering a woman describing a man watching hockey? This doesn't happen in corporate videos.

Then she says maybe we shouldn't even be talking about it. That might jinx it.

"Okay, no hockey. Tell me about yourself."

Besides "Why?", which is the best question in the world, "Tell me about you" is the other best thing to ask, under any circumstances. You could be a brilliant conversationalist and a good friend if you just use those words and nothing else.

"Well, we've been married twice," she said, looking at Mack, who you guessed is white, although he has been in the sun and the wind so long he could be any race.

"And we've been divorced twice, and I've been the other woman twice," she laughed. Mack did too.

"And now you're back together?" I asked.

"He's a glutton for punishment." They both laughed again.

"We're just friends," said Mack.

Her name is Valerie Shaw, "from Rivers Inlet," she added.

All I was thinking was, what a story. This is better than daytime soaps or nighttime reality shows about the real women of anywhere.

They met and had an affair, probably when he was married. They got married. They got divorced. He got married again. They met again and had another affair.

We are talking about a bulldog and a lioness. We are talking about two people who pulled nets from the sea. Valerie had her own boat for a while.

Then they got married again, and then divorced.

Stop. I can't keep up.

Then they met again, and they are working together as friends, sewing up the same net. When he started to say something, she finished it. When she said something, he finished it. It might drive you crazy. It probably did drive them both nuts—maybe that's why the divorces—but the bond between them is so deep you could throw the big lead weights from their boats into it and they wouldn't reach bottom.

"Do you think you would ever get together for a third time?" I asked Valerie.

"If it was worthwhile to him," she said, and then she looked up toward the other end of the net. "Look, he's listening," she said.

"Would you ever think of getting together again?" I asked Mack.

"I wouldn't want to disappoint her," he said.

"Was that a yes or a no?"

"A maybe," he said.

John took a few more pictures of them working, including her fingers, which had black electrical tape around them to keep from being cut by the lines of the net, and pictures of his hands, which were the size of hams.

Then we left.

"How did that happen?" he asked. "I mean how did we go from nothing to that?"

"Just expecting it would happen, and believing it would happen, and being thankful when it did. And luck. Simple."

Later the Canucks did win, so on television later we could point out the reason. They got help from a couple of good net minders.

35

Bagpipes, Coincidentally

In the last story I left out the part about John and me listen-ing to a bagpiper across the water after we finished the story about Mack and Valerie.

Why would I include that? No reason. It had nothing to do with the story and you don't put something into a story that doesn't belong there.

But remember, all things are connected. I think that we are just outgrowths from the earth, like leaves from a tree, and even though we can jump up we are still part of what is below us. And I believe everything is connected and we and the earth and the universe are all one thing, one living organism, and we are not separate from it, or from anyone or anything.

Of course that is all airy-fairy, hocus-pocus, meaningless philosophy. Except for the bagpipes.

John and I were standing on Fisherman's Wharf in False Creek, across from Granville Island.

Bagpipes have a distinctive sound. They can travel over water without losing their distinctiveness. You might love them, but they can also drive away your enemies. That's why they were first made. And they can drive away your wife.

I told John that I was once in the parking lot of Third Beach in Stanley Park when the cameraman and I heard bagpipe music coming from deep in the woods.

"What the heck is that?" one of us said, but both of us thought it.

We listened and we waited. Pictures with sound were taken in case something good came out of the trees, and after a short while something good did come out—a piper with his pipes.

"Hello." "Hello." The usual.

"Why? Tell us why? Why are you playing in the woods?"

"My wife hates the pipes," he said.

Shocking, I was thinking. She is also wise and sensible, I thought.

"So I can't play near her," he said. His name was Tony.

They had come to the beach and while wife and child were on the sand Tony was in the woods, out of hearing distance from the surf and the wife and the child.

He was in the woods because if he had stayed in the parking lot he would have drawn a crowd and he didn't think he played well enough for that, but he loved his pipes and he played for us and the story was funny and touching. Funny because he was playing in the woods and touching because he was dedicated enough to play in the woods. That was three years ago.

After I told the story John and I left the Fisherman's Wharf and didn't mention the piper again.

The next day another cameraman and I were in Queen's Park in New Westminster. It was Victoria Day and we were doing a story about the Ancient and Honourable Hyack Anvil Battery.

You know about that, don't you? Please say yes. I have done

a television story on it every year for the last ten years, and it was in an earlier book.

Okay, the cameraman didn't know either. Neither did the editor, and these guys I think are brilliant in every aspect of life—except BC history.

Long ago, before New Westminster was the capital of BC, in fact even before the land was called British Columbia, the folks in New West had a twenty-one-gun salute to Queen Victoria on her birthday, May 23.

That was done by the original 159-member British Regiment that was sent here to keep the peace.

Can you imagine 159 guys told to keep the peace with 20,000 Americans, most with whiskey, all with guns and all searching for gold? Those 159 guys were pretty tough.

They also had to build roads and survey the land. They weren't allowed to search for gold for themselves, and to stop them from deserting they had to wear scarlet red jackets so they could be spotted if they ran away. They had no civilian clothes.

Tough.

On top of all that, they saluted their Queen. They had a cannon and they used it, shooting out into the Fraser River, and after twenty-one big bangs they had a drink of whiskey, making it all the more fun.

I apologize if you know all this, but sadly so many don't. If you do know it, skip ahead toward the end of this story and you'll get a punchline that shocked the heck out of me.

Queen Victoria proclaimed the land as a colony to keep it from being taken over by the Americans and named it British Columbia. She was going to call it just plain Columbia until one of her top aides, who had a map, said there already was a country called Colombia. So she added British just as an afterthought.

New West was the capital and the folks were happy, partly

because Gassy Jack had a saloon in town. Fire the cannons and go to Gassy's for a beer.

In case you missed it earlier, and I know you jump around in books like this because I do the same thing, Gassy made a big mistake. Most of the residents in New West were still Americans and Gassy took a vacation with his bride. He went to Harrison Hot Springs, two days' ride away.

He left his saloon in the care of a friend, an American friend. It was the Fourth of July. After everyone celebrated the Queen's birthday in May, everyone celebrated the birthday of the USA in July.

His friend was very generous with Gassy's beer and whiskey. In fact, he gave it away.

By the time the vacation was over and Gassy was back he was broke, bankrupt and busted. This turned out to be a good thing because he uncovered his one reserve barrel of whiskey, loaded it into a rowboat and, together with his wife, brother-in-law, mother-in-law and dog, he moved around to the other side of what would become the Lower Mainland. His brother-in-law did the rowing.

There he opened a second saloon, and there was born Vancouver.

It's great to read about these guys because today if we are broke or bankrupt we go to the bank and whine. The people who gave birth to this land did neither. They just started again.

Back to New West. It lost its distinction as the capital when Vancouver Island joined the colony. Partly as a bribe to get the island to join, the capital was moved to Victoria.

Then the politicians got greedy. Surprise. The ones in Victoria also wanted the distinction of being the only place in the colony to salute the Queen with twenty-one loud bangs.

They forbade the folks in New West from making any similar

noise on her birthday. They even went so far as to take away their only cannon.

But you don't mess with New West. They were not going to be bullied, and the mayor was also a blacksmith and blacksmiths have anvils. He figured if they put some gunpowder on top of one anvil and then put another anvil on top of that and put a little spark near the powder: Bang!

The first year they did it in the middle of Columbia Street. Victoria stomped its political feet. The second year the people of New West made a bigger ceremony and blew apart the anvils twenty-one more times.

For almost 150 years they have only missed one time—1901, the year Queen Victoria died.

Now it is a ceremony with men in red coats and a brass band and it is held every year in Queen's Park, of course. It is one of the most fun salutes anywhere on earth, and most of all it shows an independence that cannot be put out. I love it. That is why I do a story on it every year.

After the ceremony this year, a sweet little lady with an English accent said hello to me. Her name was Eileen.

Then she asked if I remembered doing a story on a man who played the bagpipes in the forest.

Goose pimples.

"Yes, of course. I was talking about him only yesterday. Was he playing on Granville Island?"

She said yes.

He is her son, she said, Tony Warburton. She said he loved his pipes so much he practised until he thought he could play in public, but he worried that he didn't look the part and he couldn't afford a kilt.

So he made a sign that said, "Playing for money for a kilt" and put it on the ground in front of himself.

An old guy stopped and listened. The next day he came back with his kilt. As with many of us, the clothes he'd worn when he was younger didn't fit when he was older. The length was still fine, but the waist, well, you know.

The old fellow said he didn't want his kilt to be stuck in a drawer. He wanted it to be worn, as he had worn it in London on the day World War II ended in Europe.

That date, May 8, 1945, was inscribed with indelible ink in the waistband of the kilt.

Tony later played at the old fellow's funeral, wearing the kilt.

He wears it every time he is playing in public. He was wearing it the day before when I heard him across the water.

"I've read all your books," Eileen said. "And I buy an extra one for a friend in California."

"Thank you," I said. "I am writing another one right now. If you don't mind, maybe I could include Tony's story."

"Right now" is four hours later that same night, the night of the Queen's birthday. I still have the sounds of exploding anvils in my ears, along with the sweetness of the bagpipes across the water.

It is not a coincidence if things were meant to go together.

36

Hockey Town

If you were to shorten Vancouver's life to a week, on Monday it was a forest of giants, by Tuesday the East Side was filled with saloons and brothels and real estate agents. On Wednesday the citizens wanted hockey.

Over on Georgia and Denman the axemen were pounding into the flesh of beings that had been untouched for almost 700 years.

Hockey, they were thinking. Well, actually they weren't. They were thinking, if this thing falls this way instead of that I will look like a pancake.

Crack. It fell this way. Whoops.

Can you imagine chopping a hole in a tree, then shoving a board into the hole, then climbing up on the board and chopping another hole while not falling off the board in the first hole?

Actually, imagining it is easy. Doing it was a bummer. Sometimes they had to chop a third hole, which put them about ten feet above the forest floor.

The reason was, the centres of the ancient cedars are hollow.

That's the way nature said cedars would grow, one of the mysteries of life, like how big is the universe. But in the case of cedars, the size of the hollow inside determined how high the loggers had to climb.

The owners of the sawmills didn't want to waste their time cutting trees with hollow bottoms. On the other hand, the owners of the sawmills never had to climb up on a board to do the chopping.

By the way, the famous Hollow Tree in Stanley Park is simply the stump of a very old cedar that was hollow. No magic about it.

Anyway, the loggers would stand on a board as high as some Olympic divers climb and they would chop. Then they would saw. Then they would pray.

If you have ever chopped down a tree, you will know that the last instant before it falls is only an instant before it falls. There isn't much time between the two instants.

In the old days, once the tree started moving it was time to jump off the board. The trouble was, the other nearby trees had probably been cut down and their branches were still on the ground.

Sometimes, to save time, half a dozen trees would be half cut and then a larger tree behind them and a little uphill was cut so that it would fall on the half-cut trees.

Crash, crash, crash and so on. It must have been very noisy, and bad for raccoons and birds.

Once the logs had been sawn into sixty-foot lengths no one bothered to remove the branches from the forest floor. Sometimes the slash left behind was twenty feet deep, sometimes it was ten feet, and sometimes it was just a pile of broken branches way down there. You were way up there, standing on a skinny board, and now you had to jump before the tree you were sawing fell to the ground. Just don't slip, and don't land in a pile of branches and, whatever you do, don't break your leg. If you do, luckily it will only hurt for a few seconds before the tree falls on you.

This would never pass WorkSafeBC. "No, sir. We can't approve of loggers jumping off boards into piles of rubble while a million-pound tree is falling on them. That is against the rules."

Of course there were no rules or regulations or government inspectors or labour unions in the late 1800s. Just loggers jumping and then breaking their legs in the branches on the ground and then not being able to get away before the tree fell on them.

It made for great work opportunities for the next man wanting a job in the woods.

By 1900 the giants in the West End were disappearing like salmon in 2000. Just give us a chance and we can show those natural living things a thing or two.

The population of Vancouver was sprouting like marijuana in a modern grow op. Big houses were everywhere, partly because families were larger then but it is equally true that displays of wealth were just as important then as now.

"My house is bigger than your house." This was before Mercedes-Benz was invented. Now there are luxury cars parked out front of the tiny Yaletown condos, but it's the same mindset.

In fact, going back to then, when Shaughnessy Heights was developed for the rich, the first basic building code was that a house there had to be at least five times more expensive than the most expensive house in the rest of Vancouver. The average house had twenty rooms. Even a large family couldn't fill that, but it was good to show off.

Before Shaughnessy was created, Georgia Street was called Blue Blood Alley because all the men who owned vast tracts of the forest or interests in the sawmills were building mansions on Georgia.

All but one of those old houses are now gone. That one is

part of a towering development next door at Jervis Street. The current generation of the well-off lives in places like the Shangri-La, in condos with an unimpressive square footage but just look at that view. On a clear day you can see Nanaimo. You pay a lot to see that far.

Now they are entertained by televisions that are as wide as their walls, but back when Blue Blood Alley was thriving, the rich and poor needed entertainment. There were some theatres in the East Side, including plays by Shakespeare, but they needed something exciting and fast and heart pounding and head pounding. They needed hockey.

The city's first hockey arena was at Denman and Georgia. It was the largest one in Canada. It held 10,500 fans and most of them were there to see Cyclone Taylor.

Cyclone wasn't a star. He was a supernova. He was Wayne Gretzky before Wayne Gretzky's grandparents were born. He did things on ice half a century before they were invented. He could score backwards, or at least that is what the editorial cartoons had pictures of him doing. If he didn't do it, at least it seemed like he could.

Because of him Vancouver won the Stanley Cup in 1915.

Now, jump ahead a little. Every Tuesday morning I still meet Harold for coffee in Tim Hortons in North Vancouver. I have told you about Harold. He rode a motorcycle until he was eighty-nine. Then he tripped over his walker and wound up in the hospital. His daughter told him he would have to give up his motorcycle.

"Why?" he asked. "I tripped over my walker. I should give up that, not my motorcycle."

He is a neat guy. He was a hobo during the Depression and later became a dentist. He got the money for dental school by building houses, even though he had no idea how to build them.

That was in an earlier book. The short of it is, a friend told him how to build a house and he followed the instructions given to him over coffee and sandwiches.

His first house is still standing and still lived in. Harold, like the city of Vancouver, came from an age of don't worry if it looks impossible. He just did it.

Then one morning I was telling him about the Denman arena. His eyes brightened. He had been there, many times.

His proper Victorian aunt and mother had taken him there to hear piano concerts. Even in the 1920s hockey arenas had to supplement their income with culture, although now the concerts during off-season dates have every instrument except a piano.

And then he told me one of those things that make you leap over the years and give life to a name.

He said his dear Aunt Bessie had dated Cyclone Taylor.

"What? For real? You mean I am looking at someone who knew someone who knew an actual star?"

That is only three degrees of separation. Harold, Aunt Bessie and Cyclone. I felt like I was there watching Cyclone on the ice while Bessie was watching him. A hockey love story in the 1920s.

Cyclone was a great catch. He was famous and he had a super income. He was making $5,000 a year when the average man made less than $1,000. And he was in love with Bessie, and Bessie was in love with him. Lucky girl. Lucky boy.

However, Bessie's parents learned something about Cyclone, whom they called by his real name, Frederick (there were no crass, non-Christian nicknames in their circle), and what they learned violated their Christian morals worse than a name.

They learned that Frederick Taylor drank beer.

They forbade Bessie ever to see him again. Not even a good-bye. She never married. She died at eighty-three.

37

The Biggest Game

The seventh game of the Stanley Cup was a disaster, as you know. I watched the game with neighbours. One of them was so passionate about the Canucks that he went outside to cry when the score was three to nothing.

Then I watched the rioting at home alone.

I wanted to leave Vancouver.

That was disgusting. That was embarrassing. I used to be young and tough. I wanted to be young and tough and grab one of the kids setting fire to the cars and pound him into the ground. I wanted to be as stupid as him because I was angry, only I wanted to stop him because he was ruining the reputation of the city that I love.

However, I am not young and tough anymore, and if I were I would just have caused more problems downtown.

As for the players, they had dreamed of this moment most of their lives—their lips touching a polished piece of silver that, before this, is carried with hands that must wear gloves.

Then the unbelievable violence began. The love affair with

hockey turned into a brutal gang rape of a peaceful and beautiful city.

The rapists wanted to giggle. They wanted to show their friends that they could attack a defenceless store, rip it open and force their way inside.

They wanted to show their friends that they were tough enough to roll over cars that weren't fighting back and then kill them with fire.

They wanted to rape the small coffee shops, places they had never been inside before. Smashing the faces of the little weak stores and telling the owners to shut up or things would get worse—like telling a woman the same thing before doing the same thing.

In the recent past the people of Greece took to the streets in scenes that looked like this. The same in Egypt, but they were doing it to overthrow corrupt governments.

The kids in Vancouver had a noble calling, too. They did it so they could take pictures of themselves doing it. Look at me raping the Hudson's Bay Company.

They did it to all of us. They raped us. They raped our reputation, our dignity, our conscience, our eyes, our memories. They raped the innocence of the children who watched the game at home with their parents and then saw this. "Why are they doing that, Mommy?"

And they raped hockey. The image of the cup that was kissed that night was assaulted by a mob. The names engraved on the cup have been besmirched and dishonoured. That rape scene is now part of its life and, as with a human victim, it will never be forgotten.

And then love notes started to appear on the plywood over the shattered windows. Love notes to the city.

Love tops hate, always.

My wishing to leave was emotional. My staying is the same, only stronger.

*   *   *

I wrote the following words before the final game, when it was fun to make fun of sports. Before the smashing of the cars and the buildings I said:

> I like the name, the Stanley Cup. It is humble. It comes from one guy. Okay, he was the Governor General, who never saw a hockey game before he moved to Canada, but it is just a name linked to an exciting sport. And the trophy was originally just a punch bowl bought for $50.
>
> Then there is the opposite. The Super Bowl. Usually, not always, but usually, it is boring. There is so much hype before the game and such a letdown during it. It has gotten so bad that the commercials, which are great, are better than the game.
>
> There are more collections of Super Bowl soft drink and beer advertisements than Super Bowl highlights.
>
> All of which proves that a rose by any other name would smell as sweet—or something bad would smell as bad. Calling it the Super Bowl doesn't make it that. I like to give Shakespeare credit for most of the things I think. Shakespeare and Dr. Seuss.
>
> Shakespeare said it doesn't matter what you call something, it is the something that either gets the calling or gets forgotten. Shakespeare lived before marketing became an industry.
>
> Sports trivia question: What was the first Super Bowl called? Super Bowl I. Right?

Wrong.

And also Super Bowl II and III, same thing. They weren't called Super Bowl anything.

The organizers of the football match, which was then from two leagues, used familiar baseball terminology. They called it the World Championship Game, even though it didn't have anything to do with the world.

And not many cared. The first game between the Green Bay Packers and the Kansas City Chiefs was far from a sellout, and on television it had a bit of a fumble. The halftime commercials went on too long and when the show resumed on television the kickoff had already been kicked. Whoops.

So they kicked it again.

The next year wasn't much more exciting. Instead of improving the game, the organizers decided they needed a name, and they came up with The Big One.

It wasn't. If the organizers didn't come up with a solution, it would be hard to sell tickets to the third year of the failed World Championship and the deflating Big One.

One of the organizers was watching his kids play with a new toy from Wham-O Inc, which made the Frisbee and the Hula Hoop. It was called a Super Ball. It bounced super high and was super exciting, like all the simple ideas that came from that company.

The football team owner said, as a joke, maybe they should combine the college bowl games with the new Super Ball and call it a Super Bowl. Ha ha.

And Super Bowl III became the first Super Bowl.

The football world loved it, even though they are still waiting for it to live up to its name. It is now the largest viewed show in the US and the second-largest day for food consumption in the country, after Thanksgiving.

People in marketing say Shakespeare was wrong. A Super Bowl smells sweet because of the name. Budweiser agrees. But most comments after the game are still: "What was super about that?"

And what happened to that first game, which was not a Super Bowl? It will never be seen again. The tape was erased to record a game show.

P.S. We All Need Editors

Here is an insight that has nothing to do with hockey but everything to do with how the world could be run. Those words that you just read equating the riot to a gang rape of the city were initially written for a television essay. They were never aired. For the first time in my working life something I wrote was rejected by an editor for a reason other than spelling or being un-factual or just plain not making sense.

And now I will tell you that I think editors are wonderful. I think they are better than writers, who often think they are the most wonderful of all.

Writers think that because they have thought something it must be good, because no one else has thought it.

Editors shake their heads and think, "Heaven help us."

Saying the riot was a gang rape of the city is a harsh image. What happened was a harsh reality, and metaphorically I saw what happened as a rape by a mindless gang on a peaceful lady called Vancouver.

Then along came the editor with another image. What happens to a woman who may have suffered the same brutal attack? What happens while she is watching the horror of the street on television and thinking about the horror those words bring back to her?

She might say, please don't cheapen what happened to me

by saying that smashing cars and stores is the same thing. Please don't take the lowest, most painful, most unimaginably bad part of my life and use it as a label for someone else's stupidity.

So the editor pulled the story, and when the writer thought about it he realized, once again, that there is no end to learning about how what you say is not always what others hear.

The editor is the news director at Global, Ian Haysom, who is the strongest defender of free speech that I know. He encourages independent thought and expression, but as an editor he knows that expression, no matter how free, cannot be allowed to hurt.

As a writer I realized, once again, that everyone, in everything, needs an editor—to make sure that compassion is more than just correctly spelled.

38

Hockey Before It Was Soured

On a happier note:

While I was driving around with cameraman Roger Hope, I asked him what I should write about. I ask that of many people, because most of them are smarter than me, and Roger is super smart. He is a photographer and they all see things better than I do.

"Write about hockey," he said. It was in the early days of the playoffs.

"I know nothing about hockey," I said.

We drove on.

"Look, a Philly flag," he said.

"Where? What?" I am lost.

"On that SUV."

"What's a Philly flag?" I asked.

He looked at me like I knew nothing.

"The Philadelphia Flyers," he said one syllable at a time, just to make sure I got it.

Roger Hope was born in Canada, so he is very good at spotting the pennants of American hockey teams.

I grew up in the US. I had no idea what hockey was before moving here. I have no idea what the Flyers' pennant looks like, or even that the Flyers are from Philadelphia.

I am not a real human being, he thinks. And this was the day after the first game of the playoffs.

Roger dodged through traffic and after a half-dozen blocks and doing things that would be questionable on an ice rink, he pulled up alongside the car with the pennant and held up his Global sign at the driver. After some pointing, with just the index finger, the pennant and driver pulled over on Commercial Drive, in front of a construction site where the signs said No Stopping.

"We're not doing a story about it unless he has a good reason," I told Roger, who wasn't listening to me.

Finding a story is like finding the meaning of your life. They are both important but one is more so, only I don't know which that is. A life without a story is sad. A story without a life is impossible.

You find a story the same as you find your life, by looking for something with meaning and then doing something with it. Doing that makes you what you are and out of that come the stories.

Of course, that can also sound like philosophical gibberish and drive you crazy.

I try to look at everything, every moment, every person, every encounter, every article in a newspaper, every sit-com on TV, every argument with my wife and good time with her, and say what the heck is that about? It keeps me busy.

"Why do you have a Philly flag?" I asked the driver, who was stepping slowly out of his SUV.

Slowly, because when someone pulls you over during the playoffs because you have the flag of another team you don't jump out and say Hi.

"He should be shot," said a big construction worker who was driving off in his even bigger truck with Canuck stickers stuck all over it.

This was not friendly territory.

He stood near the door of his SUV, even though the passing traffic could have killed him. Die by fast car or die by faster Canuck fan. He stood a better chance with the cars.

"Come over here," I said pointing to the sidewalk.

"Maybe. What do you want to know?"

"Why in Vancouver do you have a Philadelphia flag?"

Easy answer, he knew. He had been asked that before. He came to the sidewalk. He spoke.

"I was born in Prince Edward Island and when I was three my father brought home two stocking caps. One was the Flyers, the other was the Canucks."

I knew in an instant he wasn't suited to be a Canucks fan. Who in Vancouver says "stocking cap"? They are toques, not caps, and not stockings.

American gangsters wore stocking caps over their faces when they went off to rob a bank or kill the members of the other gang. Stocking caps have a bad reputation.

Gangsters didn't wear toques. You've never heard in a gangster movie, "Do you have your toque? We're going to kill everyone in the Two-Fingers Mob tonight and we have to wear toques." Never. They pulled on those silly stocking caps and did their killing.

Toques are sacred. They are worn in Vancouver with a C in the middle and on TV beer commercials for Molson's with an M. Toques are made for fans.

Stocking caps are made for gangsters afraid to show their faces and for fans of Philadelphia.

"I liked the Flyers' cap better and I've been a fan ever since," he said. "Thirty years," he said.

Okay, now I like the guy. He has a deep reason for liking who he does.

"I'm a Philly's fan, too," said a voice behind me.

He was tall and had a hard hat on his strong-looking head and an unshaven chin.

This is different. If he likes Philly then bless him.

"I like Montreal," said another guy with the same kind of headwear. "Nothing wrong with liking Montreal, is there?"

Well, no.

"Chicago," said a short guy smoking a cigarette, which proved to me that they stunt your appreciation of good teams. But I wouldn't say that. The Surgeon General could be wrong.

"Calgary," said a younger guy, also with a hard hat, who had considerable strength packed into his large body.

Sounds good to me, I thought. What the heck are we going to do? Five tough guys and no Canucks fans.

"Who are you for?" the Montreal fan asked me.

I can't say no one. I can't admit I am not a hockey fan. Most importantly, I can't wimp out. I have brought the game to them and they are playing. I can't say No Fair, I quit.

They are shooting slapshots at me. They are getting ready to slam me into the Plexiglas. Game on.

"Vancouver."

"Good for you," one of them says. "They need someone."

This is the beauty of the game. That is the beauty of life. It doesn't happen the way you plan. There are surprises at every step. But you have to stand up for something, even if it's a hockey team on which you know none of the players.

When we left, Roger turned to me.

"See, you should write about hockey," he said.

He is very smart.

39

The Artist and the Ball

H e is perhaps the most dedicated artist in the world. In fifteen years he has never missed a day in putting his work on display.

In the snow. In the rain. In the sun.

"It's waterproof," he said.

It is bizarre. It is plywood shaped like birds, maybe, or octopuses, or flowers, or faces, or things that aren't like anything.

"You see a lot on the night shift."

That was Jack Proctor talking, with a glint in his eyes and dimples above his beard.

He drove a cab for twenty years, only at night. The money is generally better at night, but the danger is higher. The passengers don't often wear suits and their destination isn't the business area.

"Strange things happen in the back of a cab at night. Sometimes I wished I could see, but I had to keep my eyes on the road."

Then he quit driving and took up painting. What do you paint when the only thing you know is the road ahead, which is boring (except for idiots who go through lights), and the wild-ness behind you, which you can only glimpse for a part of a second in a mirror.

You paint the glimpses. He got a job as the caretaker of one of the beautiful old houses on 12th Avenue near Maple Street, and turned his tiny basement apartment into a studio.

What I liked best about him was that on top of his television were paint cans and in front of the screen were jars filled with brushes. No way could he watch except through the coloured bristles of the upturned brushes. That put a whole new hue on the news.

Every morning he hangs his work on frames that he's made in the front yard. His octopuses and faces and flowers spin and turn in the wind like mobiles of psychedelic dots and eyes and wings. There are always at least twenty pieces that will catch your eye, most of them wider than your arm is long.

Kids play with them and Jack doesn't stop them. If they can withstand a snowstorm, a kid spinning them only adds some beauty.

You don't have to buy. You don't even have to stop, but the first time you drive by you will do a double take. The thousandth time you will ask yourself, "Doesn't he ever take a day off?"

Nope. His gallery with no roof and no rent is open from morning 'til dark.

"It was the best experience of my life," he said, "driving a cab, at night."

Then he looked into a mirror in the middle of one of his mo-biles and his face broke into a big smile. He was the happiness inside his art.

"And remembering it is the other best experience."

As I've told you, I worked in a taxicab garage when I was a teenager—me and another fellow pumping gas into seventy cabs a night and listening to cabbies complain about everything: their pay, their tips, their customers, but most of all, about how much they hated the night shift. "Nothing good happens out there at night," they said.

According to Jack, it all depends on how you look at it.

40

Rita and Ida

I wish I knew if they were still alive and still going out together. It would be comforting to know life was still as sweet as they made it ten years ago.

We saw them sitting on a bench near Kitsilano Beach looking out at the water. Seen from the roadway, they were two snowdrops blowing in the wind. Their hair was whiter than clouds when they are puffy and billowing.

They were talking and then looking out at passing boats. Sometimes they would look at dogs being walked, but only at those dogs that get attention—the very big ones and the very tiny ones.

Hello, we said. We introduced ourselves and they told us they were Rita and Ida. They looked almost like sisters, which is what sometimes happens when you spend a lot of time, almost a lifetime, with someone else.

They met when Rita married a cousin of Ida's. That was in 1941. They have been friends ever since.

"I call her every morning," said Rita, "just to make sure she is alright."

"Do you go out for lunch?" I asked, not knowing what else to ask.

They laughed. "Every time we go out we have lunch," said Ida.

"And that is almost every day," said Rita.

They had been friends for almost sixty years when I met them. Just being near them could make you feel warm.

"We are both widows," said Rita. She said it in a way that had no self-pity.

"She was there for me," said Ida.

"And she was there for me," said Rita.

The wind blew their fine, wispy hair around. They said nothing else. Then Ida added as a side comment, "I'm just about blind. Rita tells me what we are looking at."

"I tell her a sailboat is going by and it's pretty, and then I tell her about some ridiculous-looking dog," said Rita.

We said goodbye and left. A bit of a ways away I looked back and they were still there, side by side, their white hair gently blowing, two snowdrops on an early spring day.

In truth, it doesn't matter so much if they are still there now. They would be very old now, but that is possible. The important thing is we stopped and said hello, and after ten years they still haven't faded.

41

Rolling Down the Hill

We had been through the Olympics and the Stanley Cup and the Whitecaps first season in their old stadium.

But then I saw hill rolling.

"Whatcha doing?" I asked a half-dozen kids, all maybe six or seven years old.

They had a parent who watched them after school until they went home. It was okay, he said, we could talk to them, we could find out how you do competitive hill rolling.

"We are having a contest to see who is the fastest," said a precocious girl who made competitive hill rolling sound like an important thing—which, of course, it was.

When you are six or seven, and especially if you are a girl, you have to organize things. You have to have rules. Do you think that the list of things to do when you are a husband and are handed the list by your wife just occurred to her? She has been formulating this for thirty or forty years.

The hill rolling girl went on: "You have to tuck in your arms and you have to shake your body to get going. Then you cover your face and keep your elbows in and push a little with your elbows if you can. And when you get near the bottom, push harder."

You can see her as the coach of her son's hockey team a not so long time from now. "Keep your elbows in, unless you need them to get through the crowd. Then use them, but before that keep them in. You've got a mask covering your face so don't worry about that. And when you get near the net, push harder." She was composing that list back in hill-rolling days.

I told them we would take pictures of their race. Get together at the top of the hill.

"Okay, get ready, get set. No, no, no."

One of the boys started down on "get set."

"Stop," I shouted. "I didn't say 'Go.'"

He didn't stop. His arms were out and then up. He wasn't on the coach's first string of hill rollers.

"Go, for the rest of you."

They started and it was a long hill and the girl with the tucked-in elbows was gaining. The boy who jumped the start was yelling one long syllable, uninterrupted by breathing. His arms were flapping. Her arms were tight. Her elbows were digging. His syllable was bouncing on each spin.

Most of the other kids were rolling diagonally and then slowing down, which is what happens when you pretend you are a log on a hill, because you are not a log. Your upper body is heavier and so your head starts getting ahead of your legs and you think this is not good because you can't see where you are going, so you pull your legs forward, which turns you into a horseshoe and everyone knows horseshoes can't roll down hills.

"I won," shouted the boy when he got to the bottom. Then he looked down at his feet. The girl was already there.

If someday your grandchild comes home from a sports

practice and says the coach is weird, "All she talks about is elbows," you say, "Listen to her. She's on a roll."

The father gathered up the kids and told them it was time to meet their parents, and some of the mothers are going to be mighty mad with him.

"Why?"

The one and only hazard of hill rolling: "Grass stains."

42

What Happened to the Chicks?

I know it is nearly Christmas, but we need a little Easter now.

It was just a few years ago that the chicken was just as important as the rabbit at Easter. Both were chocolate and both defied any sane connection with the day, but they were both in the race.

"My chocolate rabbit tastes better than your chocolate chicken."

"Yeah, well, my chick tastes like chicken with chocolate. You don't even know what rabbit tastes like."

This was a debate of mystery and wonderment, equal with the reason for the day. Easter is the day of Rebirth and if you are Christian it is the most holy day of the year, more than Christmas. On this day, life overcame death. If you believe it, it is the most powerful thing in life. You will be born again, or you will live forever after you die. Christians believe it. Muslims and Jews and Hindus and people of other religions believe it with some variations on how you get there.

Christianity and a few other religions latched onto the egg

as the symbol of birth. The egg is a good and understandable symbol. It is continual rebirth, no argument, but then someone thought it should be delivered by a rabbit—which became chocolate.

For years the chick, too, was living in the Easter basket, because, well, what else would come from an egg?

However, there was a time when parents wanted to add reality to Easter by bringing home live chicks to run around while their kids went hunting for eggs, which were chocolate. The animal rights people thought this was not good and asked the candy makers to cut out the chicks from the Easter parade, which many of them did. That would get the chocolate chicks out of sight and so the real chicks would be out of mind—and it worked.

That leaves only the bunny to bring eggs, which makes no sense at all, and because there were fewer chicks to look at, parents started bringing home rabbits to hop around while their kids were looking for eggs. However, real rabbits leave little brown eggs of their own that have to be pried out of the hands of toddlers before they eat them. The animal rights people didn't have to get the candy makers to stop making chocolate bunnies to protect the real bunnies. The droppings of the bunnies did that for them.

Chocolate rabbits quickly filled in the missing part of the miracle of rebirth.

And regarding eggs, if you are still colouring them at home then you are in the smallest minority. Most observant people now buy ready-made plastic eggs into which they can put a tiny chocolate bunny, knocking the chick out of the only home it can honestly call its own.

At least, and I am happy to say this, at least I haven't seen many chocolate crosses lately. Considering the pain and suffering that they caused, it would be disconcerting to see little kids chomping away on crucifixes. That could make even an atheist cringe.

And finally, the best Easter egg hunt story I ever heard came from a friend who told me that while she and some other parents were hiding eggs in a park they found a case of beer that had apparently been hidden by some teenagers. The parents drank the beer and after that they hid their eggs so well that neither they nor their kids could find most of them.

Happy Easter.

Flowers in Her Bike Helmet

She brightened up the day—she brightens up every day—but I didn't want to stop for her. She wasn't bright enough.

"Are you crazy?" Dave McKay asked.

I have written about him so much you might feel you know him. Dave is round. He has a gravel voice. He is a competitive barbecue champion. He is the lead singer in his blues band. And he tells me where to get off.

"She had feathers in her bike helmet, but not enough," I said.

He looked at me in that way that means I am too dumb for words.

"I'm stopping now and you will try to find her," he said.

"No. She doesn't have enough feathers in her hat," I said.

We are now discussing the quantity of feathers in the helmet of a woman whom we saw for three, or possibly four, seconds as she went down the street one way and we were going the other way.

"Since when did you become the arbitrator of what is and isn't the right number of feathers?" he asked as he was trying to turn around.

I was thinking that the quantity of feathers was important because it looked as though that would be all you would see in this story and, honestly, I have seen hats with more feathers than this at a recent royal wedding.

Getting the right picture is important. We had just passed by a man begging at the corner of Commercial Drive and 1st Avenue who had a pigeon on his head. He swore that the pigeon loved him—I had spoken to him before and done a story about him. He told me he had saved the pigeon after it fell out of its nest.

I half doubted that, because, honestly, have you ever seen a baby pigeon? They are unique birds that are fed milk by both their parents and they grow almost overnight into adult size. But if he says he saved it, who am I to disagree?

Then the man with the pigeon showed me the white rat that he kept in the sleeve of his coat.

I told this to Dave, who said maybe the rat had died and we could do an obituary of a rat, which might not be uplifting but would at least be different.

He pulled over and took out his BlackBerry because he was catering a large party and had to do some ordering of meat.

"Aren't you going to ask him about the rat?" he asked me.

I walked back down the street to the man with the pigeon. No, he still had his rat but he had left it home that day because it had rained and he didn't want it to get wet and maybe catch a cold.

Commercial Drive is very colourful.

I got back and Dave was using his time wisely, ordering pork butts.

"Rat is still alive," I reported.

We drove on until we saw the feathers in the helmet of the bike rider.

"Go ask her," said Dave.

Dave was the one who once stopped his truck and told me to talk to some folks who were having a picnic while their dog was sleeping under the picnic table.

I said no, they were just a family having a picnic while their dog slept under the table. Anyone could see that.

"Ask."

I got out and Dave grabbed his cell phone. That time he had ordering to do on spareribs.

I asked the picnickers. It turned out the family around the table was having a birthday party for their dog, who was now sleeping off the extra goodies. He had a cake and candles and they sang happy birthday to him.

Yes, they would sing again to their dog. Yes, they would light the candles again. Yes, they would blow them out for their dog. It would be the greatest story in the world.

"Dave!!!" I shouted.

No Dave.

"Dave!!!!" Louder. "Where are you?"

He was just finishing his order of ribs.

The story of the birthday picnic party for the dog was wonderful. Dave was right. Moral: Always take advice, even if it is meant for someone else's benefit.

This time I went into a grocery store where I thought I had seen feather helmet go. Not in this aisle, not in that aisle. I rushed from aisle to aisle because if she slipped outside while I was inside it would be like feathers blowing in the wind.

"Can I help you?" asked a clerk.

"I am looking for feathers in a helmet."

She took a step back.

"Is that a soup?"

"No, a woman."

She took another step back, but just then I saw the brightly coloured helmet moving past the opening at the other end of the aisle.

"There she is," I said as I ran. News happens fast.

"Excuse me. I hate to bother you," I said to the woman, "but could I ask you why you have feathers in your helmet?"

She tilted her head.

"They are flowers, and a bunny rabbit," she said. "No feathers."

I didn't have my glasses on.

"They are red flowers and a yellow rabbit," she said.

What I heard was wonderful, but I have a moderate degree of colour blindness and can't see reds very well, and I don't see the yellow rabbit even though I can easily see yellow.

"Where?" I ask.

It isn't easy being a professional observer when I'm unable to see a rabbit on a helmet in front of my eyes.

"Where's what?" she asked.

This wasn't going well. A stranger, me, was asking her the location of something on her bike helmet that she thought was right in front of me.

"The rabbit," I said.

She reached up, felt around and moved some of the bouquet, and there, sitting under some flowers that she said were red, was a yellow rabbit.

"Can I ask why?"

"Why what?"

"Why the rabbit?"

"I was born in the year of the rabbit."

This is too good. I ask if we can take a picture of it and put it on TV and she says yes.

You cannot find a happier guy than me. I said we would talk to her outside and she went to pay for her items and I moved quickly to the door.

There was Dave across the street, texting. He doesn't waste minutes in idle waiting.

I held up two thumbs. He grabbed his camera and in a few minutes we learned that at one time Brenda put flowers on her bike but they were stolen. So she moved them to the top of her head. No more theft.

A simple story of a woman with a problem who didn't complain about it but instead came up with a solution that also made her part of the world look better.

In a few minutes we were finished talking, Dave took all his pictures and Brenda went on her way.

"See, I told you it would be great," I said.

Two PSs. I was right about one thing. There weren't enough feathers for a story. No feathers is definitely not enough. And because Dave wouldn't believe me when I said there weren't enough feathers, he got his ordering of pork butts finished.

Never think there isn't enough of anything to do something without getting out and checking if it is there. In short, never say no without trying to find a yes.

44

The Singing Grocer

nother Dave story. It works that way with cameramen—
and with life and friends and places. You see someone or go
somewhere often, almost making a pattern, and then suddenly,
much later on, you say, "Hey, I haven't seen you, or been here,
forever, and I used to see you and be here every day."

It has something to do with how life works.

Dave told me that a grocer on Commercial Drive sings while
he works.

Who?

"Norman of Norman's Fruit and Salad store."

"Can't be," I said. "I used to shop at Norman's all the time and
I never heard him sing."

"How long ago?"

That is one of those "I go there all the time but actually I
haven't been there for years" situations.

Norman's is the vegetable store one block north of 1st
Avenue. There are rows of wooden boxes of red peppers and
tomatoes and carrots and purple onions that inch out to the

sidewalk. Everything is fresh. The air is friendly. The old Italian women wearing black and the young born-again hippies with rings through their noses shop together.

"Is Norman working today?" I asked a young lady at the cash register.

"No, his day off, but you can talk to the owners in the back, in the cooler."

The owners? Norman owns Norman's Fruit and Salad.

I go into the back of the store, past the shelves of Italian coffee and Chinese herbs, and gently open the door to the vegetable cooler.

A long time ago I was in Hong Kong doing a series on life there, and suddenly I was back there. There were four Chinese men in heavy white parkas, because it was cold in the cooler. They were sitting on boxes in a circle. I saw the same picture in Hong Kong where they were all slicing the bruised marks off onions and cutting the roots off bok choy.

"Hello, is Norman around?"

They all looked up. Everyone of them had an iPod, or an iPad, or a BlackBerry, or a hand-sized video game. There were no onions in their fingers.

"He will be in Monday," I was told.

I wished so much that I could have had a picture of what they were doing and compare that with a picture from inside my brain of what I saw in Hong Kong in the 1980s when everyone worked with their hands until they dropped.

There is no point to what I am saying except the four guys were surrounded by boxes of onions and carrots and peppers but their world was in their BlackBerries and video games.

I have been in this world for quite a while, but I don't understand it.

We returned Monday.

"No, I don't sing."

"Norman, please. I heard that you sing. I have never heard it, but I have heard that others hear it and I would love to hear it. And can I add again: Please."

"Just a little," he said.

"Tonight, tonight, won't be just any night . . ."

It was the music from *West Side Story* being sung on the East Side of town.

"That's enough," he said.

"NOOOO!" I implored.

He sang a little more and he sang to the women who came in. "Up on the roof . . ." More women came in. To be truthful, it is hard to sing to men.

"Song sung blue, everybody knows one."

He didn't have a voice that would get him on radio. He had a voice that came from his heart and it was filled with red blood cells that are filled with life and feeling and energy.

"When the moon hits your eye like a big pizza pie," he sang.

A little old Italian lady dressed in black came in. "He sings in Italian, you know."

Then Norman had the few Italian words in "That's Amore."

A Chinese woman came in. "He sings in Chinese, but I don't understand him," she said.

A Spanish woman came in. "He sings in Spanish. I don't think he understands what he is singing, but I love him."

Then a woman who had never been in the store before came in, a young, pretty white woman who was the only one in the store. Norman sang, "Tonight there will be no morning star."

She stopped stock-still at the cash register. How often do you get a song before the tax?

"I hope my husband sees this," she said looking at us and listening to him.

It was Valentine's Day.

"How come you let the fellows in the back play computer games while you do all the work?" I asked.

He smiled. "They can do whatever they want. They own the store."

What??

He said he came here fifty-one years ago and opened his vegetable and fruit stand. He worked every day—and that means seven days a week—for half a century, and then said he'd had enough. He retired.

But how do you retire from a successful fruit and vegetable store? Sell it, to the people who have worked so hard with you. He sold it to his employees.

Then Norman of Norman's Fruit and Salad got bored. He wanted to go back to work, so he applied for a job with his former employees. He now works—and sings—three days a week.

"How did you learn the songs?" I asked.

He pointed to a shelf above the ketchup. A radio, plugged into the wall and looking almost as old as Norman, was playing oldies.

"All from that," he said.

We left and listened to him from outside as he finished, "Tonight there will be no morning star . . ."

West Side Story was having an encore on Commercial Drive and a woman at the open doorway was feeling her tomatoes to make sure they were firm.

You don't need to go to the theatre to watch a live-action romantic musical. Try Norman's.

45

The Stanley Cup of Lawn Bowling

Different cameraman. This is a young fellow who has grown old. I used to work with his father before his son was out of elementary school. Yes. Maybe it is time for me to retire.

But before then we have to find a story. Mike Timbrell and I are driving in circles, as always. Taped to his dashboard is a palm-sized rock with some pebbles painted like penguins glued to it. It's a silly thing. It used to be taped to his father's dashboard.

In the late 1970s things like that were seen often. It once had a sign that said: Rock Concert. I saw it but I didn't ask his father about it. It was just always there.

Thirty-five years later I look at the same rock and the same penguins. I know it is from his father but I have never asked Mike the son about it either.

We are joking about our coffee, both black, no sugar. We are drinking it out of paper cups.

"I can taste the dirt under the fingernail of the Guatemalan picker," he says. "It has a hint of blackberry."

No wine experts are going to outdo two guys with take-out coffee.

We can find nothing to put on television. The Canucks have just moved into the finals of the Stanley Cup. The Premier wants to lower the tax rate of the HST. NATO is bombing Libya. Arnold Schwarzenegger is being universally condemned for raising two families at the same time in the governor's mansion in California, and the man who would be the next president of France is in jail in New York for allegedly attempting to rape a hotel maid.

It is hard to compete with the headlines.

It is raining on and off. Almost no one is out. Hours have gone by and we have found nothing. I am falling asleep. He gives me half his tuna fish sandwich. I bought him coffee.

"Well if there is nothing in Vancouver, let's go to Burnaby," Mike said.

That's the answer. It comes from the Bible. I have taught Mike much about religion, the good stuff. He was born on Christmas Day but he knew nothing about the birth of Jesus or the Wise Men. I told him those stories and his eyes opened wide.

He was brought up with no religion.

I told him about Easter and the Crucifixion and the burial in a tomb and the Resurrection. He was even more stunned.

I'm not saying I believe literally in all that the stories tell, but the stories are sure good. And it is amazing that someone doesn't know any of them.

But one of the parts that he likes is about moving mountains. If you have enough faith you can do that. I like that. That is basically my entire philosophy. As I've said to so many people, it doesn't mean that you can move a mountain by thinking about it. You need an excavator and government permits, and some dynamite helps, too, but if you want that mountain moved you can do it, no matter what kind of mountain it is. That means even if it's in your head, but in that case don't use dynamite.

The part of the Gospels that Mike likes best is where Jesus tells his buddy Peter how to catch fish. Peter had been out all night and was coming back skunked. Jesus hopped on board and told him to throw his net out the other side of the boat.

"Oh, come on, Jesus, if there are no fish on the starboard side there certainly aren't going to be any on the port side," said Peter.

"Trust me," said Jesus.

So, possibly just to humour his friend, Peter the wise old wrinkled fisherman tossed his net over the other side.

Bingo. He can hardly pull it back into the boat. He is swamped with fish. He is happy. Jesus is right.

I don't know if that really happened, but Jesus was right. It isn't rocket science. If something you are doing isn't working one way, try it another way. Simple.

Mike and I can't find anything interesting in Vancouver.

"Let's go to Burnaby," he said.

We were at the PNE when he said that. This means driving four blocks across Boundary Road and we will be in Burnaby, but that is the same as throwing the net out on the other side of the boat.

You could just as easily say hold your tongue on the other side of your mouth. It doesn't matter what you do, just do something else. It changes everything in your mind and that changes everything that you see and suddenly:

"What are those people doing?"

"Lawn bowling."

"During the run to the Stanley Cup," I said. "Maybe that's the Stanley Cup of rolling balls."

That is a stretch, but you never know unless you ask. So I

asked the organizer and he laughed. "Well, yes, I guess this would be the Stanley Cup of lawn bowling. It's the Men's Finals of the Lower Mainland."

He said it. Of course I suggested it, but so what? He laughed. It was facetious, but so what? We aren't looking for actual hard-core facts. We are looking for the flavours of life. We are looking for something fun that is happening now, today, in front of our eyes, that we can share with others. We are looking to get some fish in the net.

The Stanley Cup of Lawn Bowling.

"What happens when there is a big score?" I asked one spectator who was wearing a Canucks jacket.

"We clap, politely, not loudly," he said.

"What happens when one side wins?" I ask another fan.

"We say jolly good. But we keep our voices down."

And after the tournament, when hockey fans would be banging on pots and pans or their neighbour's windshield, what happens?

"We go home and warm up," said the organizer.

The net was thrown out on the other side and we pulled in a prize catch.

I'm not interested in eternal life—this one is good enough for me—but it sure makes the day better when advice from Jesus helps you find a story.

When we left I did something I had waited thirty-five years to do. I wanted to do it because I wanted to mention it in this book.

"Where did the rock come from?"

Mike said his sister had given it to their father when she was about three or four. Don put some duct tape on the bottom and stuck it on every van and truck that he had over the next twenty years, until he retired and not much later died.

After that Mike took it, and he's taped it to every camera truck and SUV he has had.

"All the trucks get turned in with a sticky part on the dash," he said. "Sorry."

You don't have to rush a good story. A good one, like a good rock, like good wine, grows better with time.

46

Street Hockey

It used to be that kids played outside and mothers did the dishes inside while fathers read the newspaper.

This was not fair to mothers, but it was an age when almost no one was overweight and fathers knew at least a little of what was going on in the world and kids slept deeply.

If you are over forty, you grew up on the street. You played tag or road hockey or hide-and-seek. Or you just walked up and down your street talking about what you would do someday when you were old enough to leave your neighbourhood.

Almost no one was inside watching television because, outside of one or two things such as *Gunsmoke* or *Star Trek*, there was nothing to watch—and those shows only ran during the fall and winter. The summer was for reruns or game shows.

But the summer was also for street games. If you were there, you were there every night. You played until the street lights came on and then tried to squeeze in a few more goals or times at bat.

Then came the computer and games on the screen. Your kids grew up playing them, staring at them, fingering them and sometimes getting remarkably high scores in the number of aliens they shot.

The games had hundreds of names and realistic characters and challenging plots. The problem was, the kids were disappearing.

At first there were simply fewer kids on the street. Then came more advanced video games and there were even fewer kids out. By the time most of us finished paying off the video games that we'd given for Christmas, which were the only thing that was on the list to Santa, there were almost no kids out. Those kids who were walking were just visiting friends to swap games.

Even the walking and the swapping took place in the dark ages before games could be downloaded and shared over the internet. After that there was no need to go outside ever, except to school, and many of the kids were being driven there.

After school the streets were empty. There was and still is organized sports practice in school yards and ice rinks, but the kids don't really play. They train, and that is sometimes not fun. They get dropped off by car, told what to do on the field and then picked up and driven home to their videos.

Then came today, Sunday, May 29, 2011, one of the best days of my current year. A cameraman, Steve Lyon, and I were looking for something, as always, but there was nothing that we liked until we saw a father pushing a baby carriage that had a Canucks flag attached to it.

Cute, but not strong enough for a story, not on its own.

A block later we passed a man in a motorized wheelchair. Flying above it was the skull and crossbones.

"Whooo, stop this camera frigate and let's look at this pirate ship," I said.

His name was Sam, he was ninety-three, and the black flag with the white skull above the crossed bones replaced his red skull and crossbones, which had worn out.

But why did he have it? He wasn't sure. He was talkative and expressive and smiling, but at ninety-three you don't really need a reason for doing things. Just doing them is reason enough.

Another man watering his lawn very close by said he took care of Sam and he had bought the flag just because it fitted with the image of the old guy.

I asked about a Canucks flag and Sam said he would get one and probably fly it above the sku!! "because if I didn't, folks might not take it so kindly."

And then we left, because I'd had an idea. Of course! That was it, a gift from the story god, the old fellow and the baby carriage. There is some connection between the two, even thought I had no idea what it was.

All we had to do was find the baby carriage and talk to the father and take some pictures, and some bridge across almost a century would be formed. Easy. Perfect.

"Which way did the father go?" I asked Steve.

"The other way," he said.

He made a U-turn. He circled one block. He circled two blocks.

"It's just a man and a carriage," he said. "We have a truck and gasoline."

Three blocks. Down that street, around the corner and up the next street.

Gone.

"Wait," I said. "Look where you got us."

Down an alley I could see some kids running around in the tennis court of a playground. I could see only part of the court and just a few kids, and I could see them for only a second as we drove by, but they were playing street hockey on a tennis court.

Beautiful.

Steven kept driving. He didn't see where or what I was talking about.

Life is like that, two people together with eyes in different directions. Sometimes that is good.

"Where are you going?"

"What are you talking about?"

I told him and he turned and there we saw uncountable numbers of kids and adults playing hockey. That may look like just a sentence in a book, the kind you'd read in school, but picture the reality of it. The tennis court was packed, legs and shoulders together, bouncing, running, flowing back and forth like a bowl filled with water that was being tilted left and right, but it was bodies, not water, and each of them had a stick and they were yelling.

That is so much better than reading there were uncountable numbers playing hockey.

"I love you forever, you know that?" I said to Steve.

He looked at me with that "Don't come close to me" look while he got his camera out.

"I mean platonically. Which means I really don't care that much," I said. "But thanks."

He shot pictures through the chain-link fence. I counted bodies. Being a reporter is easier than being a photographer. There were twenty-six people in the rink. That means there were two full teams on each side, each with two extra. That's a pretty good defence and it didn't leave much room for the tennis ball that served as a puck.

Most of all there was shouting and sticks scraping on the ground and more shouting.

Nothing, nothing in the world, could be better than this.

We went inside through the gate.

"SCORE!! We won." Someone said that, and the noise quietened down. Most of the players started leaving the court.

"Wait," I shouted. "Please, wait. Where are you going?"

"Finished," someone said. "We've been playing for more than an hour, we're pooped."

"Noooo," I said. "Noooo, please. Would you play for just five minutes more?"

"Can't," someone said. "We've had it."

"Nooooo. I can't put you on television yet. You're wonderful, but we don't have enough pictures of you playing to show how wonderful you are."

But still, "No."

A rule of life is that as soon as one person says something or does something, most others follow. It isn't always a good rule but it is true. It happens with dictatorships and with those picking up litter. It can be good or bad. In this case it was a dictatorship.

"Please," I begged. "Just five minutes more."

"I don't see any stripes on your arm," someone said.

This was going to be hard. I had no idea why but one man who wanted to be difficult was going to collapse this entire moment for some reason that was very personal to him. I guess he didn't want to be told what to do. I don't either.

I thought if I was still in the Air Force I would have stripes. I was a sergeant, and I did give orders and there was no refusing them, but that was more than forty years ago and since then I had learned you cannot order or argue a person out of or into anything that has any value.

"Okay," I said. "We're out of here."

It is strange how one story so happy can be turned into something so sad so quickly by one person. That happens in families, in jobs and in the army.

Steve was sad. I was sad. I could see some of the folks with their sticks were sad, but when one person rules it takes a movement to overturn it.

I started to walk away.

"I think we could play for a couple of minutes," someone else said. He was a man on the court with a hockey stick. He tried to be pleasant. He obviously didn't want to upset the man who'd said no, but he also obviously wanted at least to get his kids and the others on television.

And then they started playing, and for the next fifteen minutes there was laughter and scoring and running and, "She SCORED!"

"No," one pint-sized goalie shouted. "Not you."

"Who?" I asked.

"My mother tipped it in. She scored against me."

A terrible moment for the goalie, but a precious moment in life.

The parents said the game had started with a couple of kids playing and then some more joined in and then some parents came along with their sticks. They started meeting every Sunday and, except when the weather was terrible, they had played every week for the last two years.

They were kids playing and having fun, just what I had complained didn't happen anymore.

One sour parent left a bitter taste, so I did the only thing I could do. I left that out of the story. You can learn about it now because you and I are close friends and you should know all the dirt behind the stories, but on television there is no room to take away from the joy of the kids and the other parents.

Then I went home, and right on my street my neighbour, Jim Rennie, was tossing a ball to his daughter, Isobel, who had a baseball bat.

An underhand pitch, a swing, and bang—the rubber ball went over Jim's head and down the street. He ran. He got it. He came back and pitched again. Bang.

I parked my car and without saying a word went down the street behind him. The pitch, bang, over Jim's head and it hit the curb to my right. Fifty years ago when I was Isobel's age I would have snagged that. I would have taken one hop, reached out and, bare handed, grabbed that ball. Then, without a wind-up, on one foot I would have thrown a line drive back to first base. The runner would have been out by a mile.

This time I started to bend over to get the ball but some aches and pains got in the way and the ball kept going down the street. I started to run after it. My legs hurt. I walked. The ball stopped halfway down the street.

When I got there I picked it up and threw it back to Jim. It bounced a long way before it reached him.

Then Alice, who is nine, came out of her house and wanted to play and Isobel showed her how to hold the bat.

She missed the first couple of pitches, but then she connected and I again ran down the street chasing the ball.

Then Caroline, who is Alice's mother, came out with James, who is their foster child and younger than Alice. James got a chance at bat and Caroline, with a teacup in her hand, tried to play second base.

It was like it was before computer games. There was air and running and swinging and missing and groans and encouragement and yells of "car, car," and laughs and aches and pains—and I was the happiest guy on earth.

Then everyone had to go in, just like they used to long ago, and everyone, at least for a few minutes, felt the same as I did.

As for the man in the wheelchair with the skull and cross bones, we got him on television later in the week in a story about Canucks flags. It was the least we could do. Without him, nothing else would have happened.

When I came home this time, there was Alice with Kate, her

nine-year-old neighbour. They were walking together up and down the street, not out of sight of their homes. I didn't ask, but I think they were talking about what they would do when they were finally old enough to walk out into the world, just like the old days.

47

The Doll Collector

I t is one big circle. We all know that. We are born, then we die and we're buried either in body or ashes.

Then, after several million years, the leak-proof, mould-proof, eternal and expensive coffin or urn finally leaks and we are returned to the earth. That is the natural way; we just slow it down.

Then some plant will consume what is left of us and the plant will be eaten and some other creature will eat the thing that ate the plant. It is comforting to know that eventually some other life form, if there are still life forms around, will snack on us and we will join with that future consumer and be given life again. Or something like that. Either that or a computer will use our dust as lubricant.

I know that isn't the way it says it happens in the holy books, but I like it.

But that's not what happened in the case of Katherine Galan. Some of her friends went straight to heaven.

I was with cameraman John McCarron when I met her on

Powell Street. Can I detour again from the story? Every story, like everything in life, has detours and you have to have patience or you miss the story.

John McCarron and I worked together every day for years. I loved working with him. We joked and laughed and I felt like he was an extension of me, or I was of him. That was maybe because he grew up in East Vancouver and I grew up in the New York equivalent.

He is now fighting cancer. It started in his kidney and then spread to his shoulder. The last story we did together was about some flowers I had seen growing out of a hole in the concrete median on Mount Seymour Parkway.

The flowers were as beautiful as any $10 bouquet you could get in a cut-rate supermarket, but they were defying everything. They were growing where there was no dirt, except what was caught in the hole in the concrete traffic divider. They were only inches away from the moving cars that never gave them rest. The wind from Fords and Hondas and trucks and buses came in violent rushes.

But the flowers survived. That was good.

John got out his tripod because this was a difficult shot and had to be taken through traffic. We both reached out to carry the awkward three-legged camera support.

Whoops. A problem.

He had just come back to work after having one of his kidneys removed because of the cancerous tumour sucking the life out of it.

I had just come back to work after having part of my bowels removed because they were twisted and I was dying, except I didn't know it. And I didn't die.

Neither of us was supposed to lift anything over 20 pounds. The tripod was 25 pounds.

So we both carried it more than a block to the spot where he wanted to take a picture of the flowers. Picture this: two men carrying a slender tube-like object between them with two hands holding it. It was a perfect ad for a gay club.

John had gone through so much pain. His daughter was killed in a car accident while driving up to Simon Fraser University. We worked together every day for a year after that while he came to mental grips with the agony. The word "agony" isn't strong enough.

If you have lost a child you understand. If you have not, you and I don't, but John does and without any hint of doubt believes his daughter has gone on to a beautiful afterlife in heaven.

I have written about him and his hurt before. What I haven't mentioned is his good humour, even when the cancer spread from his kidney to his shoulder. He made jokes about his painful left arm. Left arm, right kidney. It's hard to keep track.

He took pictures of the flowers blowing in the exhaust fumes and then settling down for half a minute before the next rush of traffic.

The flowers whipped around, then rested, then went through another tropical storm, then slept.

I talked to several people passing by. They hadn't noticed the flowers. The few who had didn't express the same surprise I had. Without human context, flowers in a concrete divider didn't make a story. It was a picture, but not a tale.

We packed up the large metal three-legged camera holder and his camera and walked back to his company SUV. His shoulder was hurting. My stomach was hurting.

After more than thirty years, we never found a story together again, but I remember most of the ones we did find. Memory is not bad, and you don't have to carry a tripod.

He is still fighting that ugly enemy and I am out on the streets wishing he was with me—but back to Katherine, one of those stories we found together more than ten years earlier.

She was on the street on her motorized scooter and was wearing a baseball cap full of pins.

"Stop. Please stop."

The neat thing about John was that after we saw her he turned on his camera so that the beseeching of her to stop was recorded. The thrill of first meeting her was in the camera. There was no setting up in his world. He got the first reaction, which is always the best.

"Stop, please. Where did the pins come from?"

She said she had many more pins and other things and we could see them if we wanted to go to her apartment.

It was in a lower-income government-supported housing development. It looks like a prison, and I have been inside prisons.

There was a large key to get in the front door. Large keys are hard to copy, but they make you feel like a guard instead of a tenant.

And there was a large key for her apartment. Same feeling. Her door had a square three-inch by three-inch viewing hole. It was strengthened by wire in the glass. It, too, looked like a prison, a place for viewing the inmate as well as identifying the visitors.

People in subsidized housing are not treated fairly.

We went inside and there was a world of brightness and wonder and fun. First there were dolls, everywhere. There were Disneyland dolls, black dolls, white dolls and a musical wedding doll.

I picked it up. I had no right to do that but it called to me and I lifted it off the shelf over the stove.

"Don't touch that one. It's special," said Katherine. Her order was obeyed. She got her way. I put it back down and it started to play the wedding march.

"That one you can't touch," she said.

She was a protective mother-in-law. She was a mother hen. She was the woman you did not want to confront.

There were happy faces from around the world in her kitchen. There were dolls with bright dresses from world festivals in her bedroom. There were souvenirs from everywhere right here.

"Where did you get them?" I asked.

"From the dumpsters," she said. "Or from binners."

Those are the fellows who make a living digging through the garbage. Some of them knew Katherine and gave her dolls they found.

"I washed all of them and they live here," she said.

There were also coffee mugs. Five hundred of them "and no two the same. If I get a double I break it," she said.

And there were the pins, hundreds of pins hooked on dozens of hats, but not all retrieved from the garbage.

"People think I'm crazy, but I'm happy. If that's crazy, that's good."

Her phone rang: "Hello? . . . Later. I'll meet you later." She had friends.

"I was born here and I'll die here. This is where the good people live," she said.

"You were saying not all your pins came from the dumpsters," I said.

She smiled and pulled out a vest. It was covered with pins.

"This came from a lady friend. A guy who was with her conked out, if you know what I mean."

I shook my head.

"One of the ladies of the street. This fellow was with her and he conked out, you know, died, so she gave me his vest." She laughed. "She knew I liked pins."

That may not have been strictly legal, but it certainly made her pin collection grow.

Some time later, Katherine did what she said she would eventually do. She died.

The government social workers came in and started to clean out her apartment.

The dolls? Into the garbage. Twenty, thirty, seventy-five of them into the dumpster before a few neighbours heard about what was happening.

"Can we have some of them?"

No. That was against the rules and rules are important. The belongings of the dead cannot be given away unless there was formal prior written documentation. In short, there was no will. The future of the dolls was written in the rule book. They must be thrown away.

So the friends of Katherine Galen waited until the government social workers were gone and then they went through the dumpster.

Her dolls were saved, including the wedding doll. They went back into the social housing apartments on Powell Street. They stood on shelves and bookcases, and reclined on pillows on beds in many apartments.

If there is a heaven for dolls, Katherine's dolls are there. She saved her dolls from the dumpsters, and then her dolls were saved from the dumpsters again. That is like being born again in a new place.

And if Katherine, in her pauper's crematory box, is in heaven too, her last sight had to be her dolls. They would have been the angels that carried her out of this world.

The circle was complete. She brought her dolls to a new and better life, and then her dolls did the same for her.

That is the way it was written in the holy book of dolls.

48

Les Paul

On June 9, 2011, the plucking sounds of an electric guitar were heard coming from computers around the world. It was a birthday gift to a man who changed the sound of music.

The sounds came from Google, which put an image of the strings of a Les Paul guitar on its home page and made it so you could pluck them with your mouse. You can still do this if you Google "Les Paul Google." (That's a line that would have defied translation only fifteen years ago.)

If you have ever played an electric guitar or if you have a teenager who wants to play one, you know what a Les Paul guitar is. It is the holy grail of rock and roll. It is what created the sound that rock lives by.

Very briefly, Les Paul was a hard-working musician who wanted to have as many people as possible listen to him, because the more who listened the more he could afford to play music. Having a goal like that is not rocket science. It is the wish of almost everyone who makes something for others to buy. On the other hand, achieving that goal can make rocket science seem simple.

When Les Paul was nine years old he got a harmonica and learned to play it. A few years later he got a guitar and learned to play it, but he couldn't play them at the same time, so he bent some wire and hooked it over his shoulders and neck with the wire protruding in front of his face. It looked dumb—he knew that—but he could then put the harmonica in front of his lips without holding it and play both it and his guitar at the same time.

Bob Dylan used the same device to make millions.

But this is not about Les Paul's invention.

He and his wife, Mary Ford, became Les Paul and Mary Ford, all said as one name. The music they made was so different on radio that when I was young I knew older folks would stop and listen, because I watched them do that. The rest of the time you didn't stop and stare at the radio. It played music in the background and you did your work. But the sound of Les Paul and Mary Ford was not like other music. There was no way to describe it. It kind of sounded like an echo, but not quite.

It sounded that way because Les Paul was one of the first musicians in the world to use overdubbing. He would lay down one track and then another next to it, ever so slightly behind or ahead of the first. It would be a rare recording now that doesn't use this technique.

But this is not about Les Paul's techniques.

Before he was married and started recording, he wanted the people at the back of the bars and small-town dances where he was playing to hear his music. So he attached one end of a wire to his guitar and the other to the speaker of a radio. It worked. At the back of the room they heard his music.

In his late twenties he had another idea. The summary of it is he got a piece of 4" x 4" lumber, attached some guitar strings to it with a bridge for them to go over, and added a pickup. Then he ran a wire from the pickup to a radio speaker.

Wow! Now there was a sound that had never been heard before.

It looked like a log, at least a square one, so he called it The Log. It didn't look like any music instrument that he could play in public, so he took an old acoustic guitar, cut off the neck, cut the body in half and put half his log inside it. Presto. The big bang of the sound of rock and roll.

The patent he got called it an Electric Music Instrument.

As I say, folks did not walk past the radio when Les Paul and Mary Ford were on. That was a sound never heard before.

And then the music stopped.

"Did you hear? They are going to have to amputate Les Paul's arm. His right arm."

"No."

"I'm afraid it's true. The accident, you know."

Words like those were repeated across North America, and this is what they were about.

He and his wife were driving on an icy stretch of the famous Route 66 when the couple's car slipped, went sideways and then turned over—and over. Mary Ford came away without any serious injuries, but Les Paul's right arm was shattered.

It could never be repaired, the doctors told him. It would just hang like a broken pendulum. It would have to be amputated.

He said, no.

He asked the doctors if they could bend his elbow at nearly a 90-degree angle and make it stay that way. He asked if they could put pins or staples or anything in his arm so that his fingers could touch the strings of his guitar, even if his arm never moved again.

They did.

It took him a year and a half to learn how to move his fingers so that he could again make music, and then began his golden age. His most famous and beloved songs were made when his arm was as stiff as a steel rod.

If you are old enough, you can remember and hear "How High the Moon" and "The World Is Waiting for the Sunrise." You can do this without a CD—you can just remember it, because when Les Paul and Mary Ford made music it was unforgettable.

And those songs, along with a long list of others, were made after the world and the doctors thought he would never play again.

49

Stolen Bike

We were looking. We are always looking. I begin most of these stories with "We were looking."

I begin most of my family stories with "We were looking."

My biggest granddaughter says, "Yes, I know, you were looking. Please, just tell us what you found."

It is humbling. A seven-year-old is wise, like a Hollywood director. "Cut to the chase. The chase is what they came to see. Go to the chase scene."

Instead, "we were looking." That is boring. I would close the book if I read that again. Ruby, my oldest granddaughter is right.

What we found was great. We saw a boy walking on a log. What better thing could you hope for? A boy on a log.

I asked his parents, of course, if we could take his picture. Yes, of course.

"How can you be such a good log walker?" I asked.

"I use my brain and my legs." His name was Evan (I asked him that). After that he left me in the dust.

This is a seven-year-old saying he uses his brain to walk on a log.

If I had a log when I was seven and someone asked me how I could walk on it I would have said, "Are you one of those men my mother told me not to talk to? I've heard people like you hang out around logs waiting for kids to walk on them."

Or I would have said, "What do you mean, 'How do I walk on them?' I put my feet out and I try not to fall off."

Answers were simpler before this kid's parents were born, that is before the internet.

"What do you mean you use your brain?"

In one flash of incredible excitement I am the happiest guy on earth, once again. This boy has said something that is way beyond me and therefore way beyond some of the audience.

I always figure I am like the audience, and if I don't get something then they, meaning you, won't get it. A long time ago I felt like I was part of you and basically I was you. How you felt, I felt. How you believed, I believed. That was when I realized that was as deep as I was going in life. If I am like you and you are like me, there is no point in ever getting angry or not understanding someone again.

When you cut me off getting off at the next exit, I think, I might have done the same thing. No anger, no blood pressure surge. We are all in this together and we do stupid things and we do amazing things. Thank you, I understand.

"I think of nothing," he said.

That is kung fu, I thought, that is Buddhist philosophy, and it's coming from a seven-year-old.

Thank you.

He walked the log. We had pictures. I was happy. It is a very simple existence.

"What do you want to be when you grow up?"

I always ask that question of kids. It usually gets an eye-opening answer.

"A scientist," Evan said. "I have a microscope and I look into it and see little germs."

But before he finished I saw that the god of all things had just ripped open the duffle bag of kindness and amazement and life. Coming toward us was a little girl, balancing on the same log.

Girl. Boy. Thank you.

She walked up to us. Her name was Alexandria. I asked Evan what he thought of her walking.

"She's very good."

In ten years he will meet someone who will be walking on the sidewalk and he will say she is very good. She will breathe and he will say she does that very well. She will smile and he will say she does that better than anyone.

But for now, "she's very good" at walking on a log is good enough.

As in life, she turned around and started walking away. As in life, he started to follow her.

A few logs later she slipped. The log was wet. She banged her knee.

"Oh, no." Whether or not I am watching, I don't want anyone hurt.

"I'm okay," she said.

Evan checked her knee. I was bubbling. Love. Scraped knee. A boy who uses his brain. Tell me one thing that could be better?

And then Evan's parents had to leave.

I asked Alexandria her age.

"Five," she said.

"No, six," said her father.

"Yes, six the day before yesterday."

Alexandria's father said it was time to go. She walked the logs all the way to the end of the beach and then ran off and tripped on the sand. Her father picked her up.

I was so happy I could have burst. Real life with things happening right in front of me. Falling on the sand, getting picked up. It doesn't take much. It is like watching a puppy or a kitten. They do nothing but flop down and then get up again, and we cannot close our eyes. A girl who is six years and two days old falling on the beach and then being helped up by her father is the same. You watch and smile.

Later, in the parking lot when we were leaving, I saw Alexandria and her father again, but something wasn't right. They were carrying bike helmets, but they had no bike.

"What's up?"

Someone had stolen his bike the day before. The father and daughter had come back to the beach to look for it.

"Someone needed it more than we did," said Alexandria.

Parents always tell their kids that when they have been ripped off. It softens the hit.

"But we really needed it more than they did," she added.

Right on, girl. You did need it and, more than that, it was yours. And they didn't need it, except to support a costly habit of injecting stuff into their arms to make them feel good. He or she was a miserable, hurtful person who waited until you and your father went into Mac's to get an ice cream and then grabbed your bike and ran.

If you have ever had something taken from you, you know how it feels. You still feel it now, years later. I know. I still feel the emptiness of going into an apartment house to get something and coming out less than a minute later to find that the bicycle I relied on to get me everywhere was gone.

And you remember the empty moment when you see that what you had isn't yours any longer.

Darn. Or worse.

You tell your six-year-old someone else needed it more, but it doesn't work. You have to walk.

"We can't go anywhere without our bike," said Alexandria.

I did a story about that. This is the kind of theft that the police stories should be about—the theft of a bicycle and what it means to a father and a six-year-old.

If we could stop those thefts there would be fewer stories about the theft of cars and million-dollar stocks.

I said on TV that if anyone saw someone turn up with a black mountain bike with an orange seat in the front for a young girl they should do something—call us, call someone, do something.

You can't let someone get away with that, or they'll do it again.

Within an hour the bike was probably on East Hastings near Carrall in the "Market." That's where the drug addicts and the thieves and the street people gather to sell the items that they have "found" overnight. It shouldn't be allowed to be there, but it is.

Anyway, the next day I got calls from several people who wanted to help. That was good of them, very good, but I always have the feeling that there are so many people in need who don't get on television and the next day they still have their need.

However, Alexandria *was* on television and the next day someone dropped off a $500 gift certificate at the front door of the television station for a new bike.

Oh my gosh.

Several other people called and offered to buy a new bike.

I called the fellow who was the victim: Dennis Beckrud.

"I couldn't take the money." he said.

From that moment I liked him.

"I couldn't profit from my loss," he said.

I liked him more.

"But I have this gift of $500," I said.

"You could give it to a charity."

I can't like him more. It is impossible.

"But I don't know who the $500 came from," I said. "There is no way they will ever know what happened to their gift."

"If you did give it to me I would turn it into five bikes for foster kids," said Dennis.

Okay, it is possible to like him even more.

Dennis works with a foster care organization and he wanted to help them. He was the victim. He was the one I felt bad for. He was the one others wanted to help. And now he was the one helping others.

It is impossible to predict how good life can be if you want to make it that way.

The moral?

Why does everything have to have a moral? I guess because that is the way I was brought up. Every action ended with the words: "And the moral of that is?" because we were supposed to learn from everything, especially things we did wrong. That's why it ends with a moral.

The moral was: If you see a boy balancing on a log, it could lead to helping some foster kids get bikes, proving that life is impossible to predict but not so hard to make good.

50

Can't Have Things, So Have Things

Wally and Leona Hobson had a beautiful veggie patch. It was in front of their trailer in Maple Ridge. They loved it.

It's gone now. They are happier.

Alfredia Wagstaff had a blue-ribbon-winning dog. She loved it but, like the vegetable patch, it is gone. She is happier.

We all hate to lose things that we love, but often things get better—if we work on it.

"We had lettuce and tomatoes and green onions, everything," said Leona. "And it was right in front of our trailer. All we had to do was step outside and gather up dinner."

You can't beat that. "And then the cats came," she said.

"All those nice raised garden boxes that we filled with soft dirt attracted every cat in the neighbourhood. I wasn't going to eat anything that came from that dirt."

Sadness. Disappointment. We have all been there.

Move to a different time and a different place. I was at a dog show in Abbotsford. For those of us who don't understand how much time and money can be put into a creature that is descended from the fearless wolf, dog shows are a mystery.

There are breeds with long names and short hair. There are breeds with long hair over their snouts and basic military cuts behind that.

One woman kept stroking her dog's tail so he or she would hold it straight up. She stroked. It flopped. Stroked again, flopped again. She sprayed something on it. It stayed up.

You could hear the laughter in the wolf den.

Watching from the side was Alfredia. She was in a wheelchair and had been brought here by her extended care home for an outing.

She had a floppy white dog in her lap. It still had the price tag on it.

"I used to have Peppy. He took the ribbon away from a woman in Burnaby. She was so mad."

Alfredia was so happy when she said that. She repeated it and was even happier.

That could have been half a century earlier, or more. Peppy could have been her first dog or her tenth. I don't know.

What I did know was that she was happy with the memory.

"This one is like Peppy," she said. She had bought him at the show. She stroked his ears. "I can have this one in the home, and I don't have to use a . . . (her voice went down to a whisper) . . . a pooper scooper." She smiled. That was obviously a word she was not raised to say, and now she would never have to use.

Back at the garden Leona pointed to her beer keg filled with plastic flowers, and Snoopy made of milk jugs.

"There are no weeds and no cats," a neighbour said.

The neighbour also told us she gets a laugh every time she passes the garden or tells someone else that she lives next door to the only legal non-medicinal pot plant in Canada. It was a pot on top of a metal plant.

There was also a rusty toy truck with non-rusting plastic flowers, a bird made from the head of a broken shovel and an airplane constructed of empty pop cans.

"It's not a garden of eating, it's a garden of not working," said Wally.

They had to buy their vegetables now, but there was no way they could purchase the good feeling they gave to themselves in their garden of toys.

"Which is better?" I asked at separate times of both Leona and Alfredia, "The old or the new?"

Neither one answered. It was not a contest. What they had was good. What they have is good. What they did not have was regret.

51

The Ice Cream Cone

He wanted to sample everything. That's the way Karl Cassleman eats and lives.

We had just finished finding and recording a story about a young man, David Tran, who had Vietnamese ancestors, making Mexican tacos two blocks from one of the giant TV screens near the CBC. The crowds had not yet arrived. He was waiting and knew he would be sold out in minutes.

"I have been on TV so much," he said.

Since the start of the hockey playoffs, reporters from all over the US and Canada had interviewed him. It was a no-brainer, which fits perfectly with many reporters. He was easy to find and he had food.

We did the same. David was working his way through university, taking a master's degree in architecture.

Great, I thought. Please give us a review on some nearby buildings. The Hydro Building right behind him.

"The top few floors are supposed to look like a waterfall," he said.

I had never seen it that way and after he told me what it was supposed to look like I still couldn't see it.

I asked him about the new retractable roof on the old stadium. This time I saw what he saw: "Scary and an invitation to aliens."

This guy is great, I was thinking. Witty, bright, knowledgeable, friendly, and then from behind me, "That smells very good," said Karl, holding his camera and getting distracted.

The tacos were frying and Karl was interested. To make them different from other tacos they were topped with kimchi, which put a layer of Korea over Mexico.

As soon as we finished working Karl ate three of them, with extra topping and a juice drink. We said goodbye and drove all of four blocks before he pulled over in front of the International House of Ice Cream.

I have written about that place before, but here's a recap. Karl says that of all the stories I have told him, this is his favourite. I say, of course—it's about food.

A long time ago I went to a sports bar just off the main part of Commercial Drive. This was just at the birth of sports bars, when they had satellite receiving dishes that were big enough to make a roof over a small house.

The problem with this sports bar was that there was almost no one watching the sports coming in on the satellite. That was because the bar's location was just off the main part of Commercial Drive.

Real estate agents are right. Location is almost everything. Having bread baking in the oven while you are trying to sell your house is actually better than location, but the sports bar had no bread and no location.

The bar belonged to Vince and Pina Misceo. They went out of business. They were a young couple with very young children and no money. The only thing they could think of doing was selling gelato from a booth at the Pacific National Exhibition, which was due to open soon.

They built the plywood stand and they made their own ice cream. And they had lineups. They were so successful that they soon opened an ice cream store literally one step from the railroad tracks that cross Venables Street a block from Clark Drive.

It doesn't matter if you can't picture it. Some day you will drive by and see a bright pink box of a building. You will then picture it forever. The International House of Ice Cream will be there until you return on a hot summer night and wait in a lineup to chose from more than 200 flavours.

The work goes on in the back of the store, mixing up new flavours, and money keeps pouring in the front.

"But you CAN'T eat more," I said to Karl.

"Got to," he said. "I can't pass the place without tasting something new."

This is the guy who has memorized most of the menu in half a dozen Chinese restaurants.

"Well I can't," I said.

"You must," he said.

I went inside to say hello to Pina.

"Take a sample," she said.

"No, thank you," I said.

Then I heard the tapping of a coin on one of the counters behind me. That is what makes a day perfect. Something happened.

There was an ancient Chinese man in an overcoat and a hat standing at the counter in front of Sonjia, who had married one of the sons of Vince and Pina. The man could barely reach the top of the counter but he kept tapping his coin. She kept asking what he wanted. He kept tapping. She kept asking.

Sonjia shouted across the store to Pina, "Do you know what he wants?"

"Give him a scoop of durian," said Pina.

"But he only has a toonie."

"Give it to him anyway." Pina is not just Sonjia's mother-in-law—she is also the boss.

Sonjia opened the back of a display counter and reached in with a scoop. Then she quickly pulled her head out.

"Ugh," she said. "That is awful."

How can ice cream be awful I wondered?

"Hold your breath," said Pina.

Sonjia gave the old man a scoop of durian ice cream for less than half price and he left licking his cone. Karl and I watched him go down the three stairs by the door. He held his cane in one hand and tried to hold the railing with his other hand, but the hand with the cane also held the ice cream and he was licking it. You can't wait when you have something you want and it's in your hand. We watched, ready to grab, in case.

"Here, taste this," said Pina to Karl. She gave him a tasting spoon of durian.

He licked. "Oh, god, that's terrible. It smells like dirty old socks."

Pina told us that durian is the true dividing line between cultures. It comes from Asia, mostly Indonesia. To Asians it is the King of Fruits. Before it is cut up it looks like a small football covered with spikes, but the smell inside the fruit is repulsive and stomach-turning—that is, if you are a westerner. If you are Asian it is heavenly and incomparable. It all depends on what you grow up with.

It is the best selling fruit in Asia, but with tourism being so important, some hotels in Indonesia that cater largely to westerners have signs up that forbid bringing durian fruit into their rooms. The smell will drive away the tourists.

She gave me a taste. I couldn't get it down.

Then Pina told us something that lets you know about demographics in Vancouver better than the Census Bureau.

"Durian is our best-selling ice cream," she said. "Number one, primo, and I can't stand it."

"Can't be better than chocolate," I said.

She nodded. "Easily beats chocolate."

Vancouver was once aboriginal. They smoked salmon. Then it became English. They fried bacon. Now it is predominantly Asian. Durian.

Some day some Asian friend will offer it to you. Be warned. Be polite.

Karl and I went outside and there was a prize-winning picture: the ancient man in his overcoat and cap, stooped over, leaning on his cane in the hot sun, licking his ice cream cone. He could have been ten years old.

And the only reason I got to savour that moment, which was sweeter than chocolate, was because Karl wanted dessert after his Mexican tacos, which is still hard to believe.

52

The Vacation Home

Mike said the words I was hoping to hear, but I didn't know that until he said it.

"I want to be here, in my garden," he said.

I had asked where he would like to go on a vacation.

"I went with my daughter to Hawaii. We were in a hotel. It was nice, and I love my daughter, but I wanted to be in my garden."

This isn't like the trendy idea of the Staycation, where you stay in BC and explore. That's a good idea, too, but that's still an outward-looking process, seeking fun or adventure. Mike wanted to be between his rows of beans.

"I have a lot of pain," he said. "I had a heart operation and some other things, but when I come here nothing hurts."

Mike Caldarone is seventy-eight. His garden is a rented plot in South Burnaby. On it he has built a tool shack, which leaves just enough room—about twenty square feet—for a bench that can seat two.

"I hate to ask," I asked when I was with him inside his vacation home, "and you don't have to answer, but what are these glasses for?"

I took a small tumbler off a shelf. There were only two shelves in his shack, one with jars of beans for planting and one with glasses.

"I apologize, I have only a little."

A little what?

He reached down into a little space between two boards near a wall and pulled out a bottle of red wine.

"It's my medicine. I only drink a sip. This bottle will last two weeks."

He offered me some.

"No, thank you, I'm working. Did you make it?"

"I'm Italian; of course I made it."

It is probably against the rules of the community garden to have alcohol there, but in Mike's defence it is not alcohol, it's medicine.

He was disappointed that his wife was not there to join us. She would be coming later, he said. They have been married fifty-nine years.

"We went to school together. We grew up together. We stay together."

Now there are two things I want to do: have only a sip of wine a day and stay married.

I told him that when we came to BC and I was working at the *Vancouver Sun* I rewrote a press release story about the creation of community gardens. The first one was to be in South Richmond.

"This would be great," I told my wife. "We could grow corn and beans and potatoes and—what else do you grow?"

You know this already, but I grew up in New York, and the only thing we grew was . . . Wait. I was going to name something ridiculous as an example of the only thing we grew, but we didn't grow anything. And nothing grew. Grass? Forgetaboutit. Trees? They were in the storybooks in school. Fruits and vegetables? They came in cans.

"You know nothing about growing anything," my wife said.

"I can learn," I said.

"Where is this place?" she asked.

"About an hour's drive from here."

We lived in Lower Lonsdale in North Vancouver before it became trendy.

"But it's only a couple of trips. We just plant the seeds and then we go back later and harvest our meals."

She looked doubtful, but shrugged. I didn't play golf. I didn't have bowling nights. Gardening, she knew, would be something I would start and then lose interest in and abandon. A temporary reluctant shrug is sometimes much wiser than a permanent "No."

The garden was just off Highway 99 on Steveston Highway. It was a large, abandoned field that once grew something but now was left with nothing but thick roots under the ground that didn't want to come up above the ground.

For the first weekend, we made one round trip per day, one hour each way. We dug and pulled and broke the shaft on a pitchfork that I didn't know I would have to buy, along with owning for the first time in my life a shovel and a hoe and seeds and a hose.

"Where do I attach this?" I asked another farmer working on his twenty- by sixty-foot farm.

"There's no water here," he said. "You have to get it out of the ditch over there."

The drainage ditch ran around the edge of the land and it was "over there." Except that "over there" meant "WAY over there."

My kids thought this was fun—for about five minutes. They

got a plastic bucket and a rope and came back with a half-filled bucket and totally soaked pants, shoes and socks.

The short of this is that we drove back and forth every weekend, both days, for the entire spring, summer and fall of our first year in Canada. One time, after our car was wrecked while it was parked by the curb, I had to rent a car to get to the cucumbers, which were not doing well because cucumbers need a lot of water. This I did not know.

My car was wrecked on Grey Cup weekend when someone driving under the influence of football excitement missed seeing the fact that my car was parked. I didn't even know what the Grey Cup was. Despite that, I have been a fan of Canadian football ever since. It really is better than American football, but it needs a better public relations department.

We got beans, and a few tomatoes and carrots that looked like crooked sticks, having grown around the roots that refused to come out. And I have one picture. This is a real photo on photo paper, not in a computer. It's on my desk. The colours are fading. It has a very proud woman and two kids who were much shorter than her standing in front of a row of corn.

It was the best vacation I had ever had.

That garden later became Bill and Lillian Vander Zalm's Fantasy Garden. They had owned the land and we cleared it for them. That was a fair exchange. We got to keep the memory. The garden plots are now a parking lot.

But I knew what Mike Caldarone was talking about when he said he would rather be in his garden, his rented garden plot, than a fancy hotel anywhere.

I did a story about him on television and ended it by saying that his vacation was at the perfect time in the perfect place.

That is one of those television lines that pretends to be meaningful, but it was as close as I could come to being honest with a deadline just ahead. The story was being edited and I was writing it on Georgia Street in one of the mobile editing trucks while the next reporter was waiting to do a court case that was breaking at that same moment. So, be quick Mike and say something bright.

What I should have said is a vacation is where you want to be, and when you are there you are always on vacation. And when I look at that photo on my desk, especially after visiting Mike Caldarone, I realize that the perfect place is more than near a drainage ditch in South Richmond or a tool-shed condo surrounded by beans in South Burnaby. The perfect place is in your head and your heart. It is you who makes the place perfect.

53

Fence Post Hole

Everything in life depends on how you look at it. You know that. I know that. I live by that. If you look at life as being good then you see it as good. If you look at it as cruel and smelly then that is what you get.

But sometimes it goes deeper than that. This is one of those cases of looking at something from the other side and, bingo, you save the day.

We were watching a man digging holes for fence posts. It was cold and raining, so no one was overly happy. The digging was in a rough spot, in a vacant lot that used to be a biker bar on Main Street, just a short walk from the old CN rail station.

The digging was hard because the ground was filled with broken concrete. I could see the pain each time the fellow drove his post hole digger into the ground and it hit something immovable.

Cameraman Mike Timbrell and I talked to him for a while. His name was Ernie Cote and he had a Quebec accent. He was pleasant and said these old demolition sites were among the harder jobs.

Then he drove his two-handled digger into the hole again and we heard it clang against something that he would have to dig out with a shovel.

He told us the fence had to go up to keep the homeless out of the vacant lot. Then he pushed a shovel into the hole. Whatever was stuck was stronger. He used a crowbar and fought with the obstacle down below.

I liked him, he was friendly, and I know it is always good to show someone working hard because the men at home can say to themselves, I could do that, and the women can say to themselves, I wish my husband could do that.

On the other hand, watching someone digging holes to put up a fence to keep poor people out would just leave me saying, "Why am I watching that?" I am an astute critic of me. There was nothing deeper to learn about homelessness or the old bar or building fences.

Mike and I wished Ernie a good day and left. We had walked halfway across the street when Mike said, "I bet he doesn't worry about getting fat."

What??!! Of course. The obvious, right in front of me, and I missed it. This is true with every single thing in life. Look at it differently and you will get a different view, duh.

Before I could tell Mike that I loved him I made a rapid U-turn and almost ran back to Ernie.

"Were you ever fat or overweight or in bad shape or anything like that?"

I didn't want to miss any of the key words.

"I lost 80 pounds doing this," he said.

OMG. There is that new way of talking again, but I meant it.

"What did you weigh, and when, and how long did it take?"

He said that a dozen years ago he weighed 250 pounds. Then

he got the job putting up fences, which meant digging a lot of holes.

"In a year I weighed 170 pounds."

This is the universal good news story. It doesn't matter that he has to do the impossible to lose weight. He lost it, and that is all that matters.

"What do you eat?" I asked, because I know proper eating has something to do with weight loss.

"Lasagna, I love lasagna."

He said he would make a lasagna in a 12-inch baking dish. "Then I put in two packages of cheese. I love cheese."

"You mean the whole package, two times?" I know cheese is fattening.

"One package of mozzarella and one of cheddar."

"And how long does that last you?"

"Two days."

He lived alone. He made a dish of pasta and chopped meat and cheese for himself every week. On other nights he had steak and potatoes, and chicken. The chicken would only last one night. And he had casseroles made with leftovers.

He broke other rules, too. He would eat and then watch television and go to bed. And he drank beer, only beer, but he drank at least two a night, except on weekends, when he drank a few more. And there was a large breakfast every morning and a lunch of sandwiches and cake and pop and a few snacks.

And he lost 80 pounds.

All it took was digging holes.

Of course, there wasn't a person in the audience of way more than half a million people who would go out and dig a fence hole, but the reaction to that story was huge. Almost everyone who wrote or called thanked him and me for reminding them that exercise is the answer.

I don't know why we have to be reminded of the obvious. Then again, I don't know why I had to be reminded that if I look at something differently it goes from washout to the winner on the Biggest Loser.

Forget the diets. Build fences.

54

Laughing Hand

I t is such a cliché: You cannot judge a book by its cover (except for this one) and you cannot judge an artist by his ball.

He was painting, and a large, round, rusty fishing weight was hanging by a chain from his easel.

That's good enough for me. Any artist who keeps himself steady with an old piece of iron is very artistic and, better than that, he has something for us to take a picture of.

As we made our way toward him I thought of the history of the fishing weight. It had probably spent a long time under the ocean holding down nets. Maybe the artist had a friend who was a fisherman. Maybe he was a fisherman. Either of those or some other story would be good.

We started taking pictures and talking and he was pleasant. He had a rugged face with many lines. Probably he was a fisherman.

He was painting the Sunrise Market, at Gore and Powell Streets. That was an odd thing to do a painting of, I thought, but artists are odd people.

"Why do you have the fishing weight?"

He looked at me like I wasn't too bright.

"To hold down my easel." He didn't say that should be fairly obvious.

"It looks very rusty," I said.

"That's because it's a fishing ball." He didn't say that that should also be blatantly obvious.

"It's sort of romantic," I said desperately. "It must have a neat story behind it."

"I haven't got a clue. I found it."

Then he went back to painting.

I don't like doing stories on artists, because I don't understand most art. I also don't understand most artists, because I'm not sure if they are being strange because they are artists or being artists because they are strange. I am a terrible judge of artistic character.

The artist in this case said he levitated when he painted—and I thought, I'll just take a step back.

Then he told me to take a look at his picture of the market. "See, it looks like I am standing about ten feet off the ground and looking down."

That made sense, but not a story.

He told me that he named his hand, his left hand, the one that did all the work, Laughing Hand. That was weird, but still not a full story.

Then he told me that painting freed him from the earth and he felt he was on a different plane when he was creating. I have heard this from many artists and writers. It happens to me sometimes when I am sitting at a keyboard and getting into the world of someone else, and I realize after a while that I am not where I thought I was. I am actually in a different world. As soon as I realize that, I crash back down into this world.

However, that is impossible to explain in a television story. Actually, it is impossible to explain in any story and it would sound weird to anyone who hasn't experienced it. If you were looking at a man painting and I said "He sometimes feels like he is on another plane," many would say, "and what drugs is he taking?"

So skip that. This was not going to work. I stepped further back and apologized for interrupting him and said we would stop bothering him and he could get back to work.

"Would you like to see some of my paintings?" he asked.

Oh, gosh, no, I thought. I don't want to look through your work and smile and not understand it and spend more time when I should be out looking for something that fits into the brief, the blunt art of television.

"Sure, I would love to," I said. I followed him down the street to an old brown van. Hanging on the side of it, like on a wall in an art gallery, were a dozen of his paintings.

Oh, heavens. "This is you? I mean, these are yours?!"

He looked at me again as if to say how could I ask something that should be obvious. He was showing me his paintings and I was asking if they were his.

I had seen them all before in a book and in newspapers. They were of the history of the East Side. They were paintings of The Only and the pink neon pig on Save-On-Meats on East Hastings, of the Penthouse and the Blue Eagle Café, and the Brandiz and Cobalt Hotels when they were swinging places.

And there was one of Vie's Chicken and Steak House. I used that picture to inspire me when I was writing a history of the black community in Vancouver. Vie's was the place for soul food and for the only meal you could get in town if you were black.

Oh, sure. You could eat in other restaurants, but in truth, if you didn't want to go through the hassle and indignities and spilled coffee, you went to Vie's. It was just off Main on Prior Street in Vancouver's only black community, which doesn't exist any longer. That story is earlier in this book.

The house next to Vie's was where Jimmy Hendrix stayed and played with his guitar while he was visiting his Canadian grandmother, who worked in the kitchen.

Just as a side note, I learned while I was writing that story that Jimmy Hendrix, who was one of the world's greatest left-handed electric guitar players, was not left-handed. He figured the hand fingering the strings had to do most of the work so he swapped the strings and had his right hand do that while he strummed with his left. If you heard him play the US national anthem at Woodstock you would know one thing. He was one of the world's greatest electric guitar players, regardless of which hand he used.

"You painted these?"

"And more."

No more levitation, just Vancouver's East Side, which is overloaded with rich cultural history from loggers and boozers to jazz and fried chicken.

His name: Keith McKellar. His history: he was homeless in Vancouver in the 1980s. He did many jobs, but found painting. He pulled a wagon around town for years, setting up his easel and doing pictures of the Sun Tower, the Eagles Club, the Smilin' Buddha.

"I did a story once on Igor, the bouncer in the Smilin' Buddha," I said. I said that half out of excitement, because here was someone who also loved the rough past of the city, and half to let him know I have been around, at least a little.

"I knew Igor well," said Keith. "He was hit by a car and that ended his career."

Whoops. Here was someone who knew Vancouver better than me.

And there was the Penthouse. I told him how I got to be a friend of Joe Phillliponi, who was the Godfather of Vancouver from the 1940s through the '70s. He had a long reign.

And I told him how Joe and I would have coffee, because he didn't drink, in his Penthouse. That was a second-floor apartment above the office of his taxi company where he would have late-night friends come and visit. The second-floor apartment turned into a nightclub, called the Penthouse. It spread to the garage below and became one of Vancouver's most infamous and bawdy night spots.

This is an old story, told many times before, but it is my favourite story of all my time in Vancouver.

Joe and I had became friends. He told me stories of old Vancouver and of trying to be the older brother who was supporting the entire family. He had gone from coal mining to nightclubbing. Some of what he did was legal. Some might not have been.

During the times of harsh liquor laws in Canada he had spotters on the roof of his nightclub. When they saw police approaching they would push a button that would ring a bell downstairs in the club and everyone would take their bottles of scotch and gin and slip them into metal holders under the tables.

The police would come in, look around, get a small donation to the policeman's ball, and leave.

Joe would also charge the prostitutes who used his club, but the only cost was the two dollars entrance fee. They would pay, meet someone, go away and do whatever it is they did, and then return and pay two dollars more.

The police eventually put him behind bars for living off the "avails of prostitution," which I thought was really stretching the law to make a point.

While Joe was running his business there were no drug-crazy

hookers on the street. The women of the night worked out of his ground-floor nightclub, and at least they were safe and warm and dry between jobs.

Not now. The poor women are on the street, shivering in winter and terrified every night. It was better with the Penthouse.

Joe went to jail for a few hours. It was enough so the police could say they got him. After that he said to me that he had a clean show of country music coming up. "Bring your family," he said.

You do not bring your family to the Penthouse. Ever. This is not Disneyland.

We arrived on time. There was a lineup. There was always a lineup for the Penthouse, no matter what the show.

We stood at the back of the line—me, my wife and son and daughter. It was an interesting crowd. There were high rollers and nightclubbers and seductively dressed ladies and men who looked like they wanted to look like gangsters.

My kids held my hands.

I knew Joe could see everything going on outside by an ingenious concoction of mirrors.

In a few minutes he came out of his apartment. The crowd looked up. Joe was making an appearance.

"Joe." It was always "Joe." No one said "him" or "he." It was "I saw Joe," and, "Joe, you know Joe, Joe told me ..." "that was Joe I was talking with." No one wanted it to be missed that he was talking about Joe.

Joe came down the stairs and Joe waddled out onto the sidewalk. Joe was not fat. Joe was round like a bowling ball and just as hard. Joe waddled out past the crowd, which parted for his passing. No one would get in Joe's way but everyone wanted to say, "Hiya, Joe." They held out their hands, hoping to be touched.

He ignored them. He walked to the end of the line where we were standing and politely said hello to my wife.

Joe wasn't dressed like those on his line. They had sharp clothes. He had a checked jacket that didn't fit, over a striped shirt that was too small, with a bright tie that was too wide.

No one noticed.

He took my son and daughter by the hands and walked them past the line to the front door. Inside, the place was already filled. He took them to the front of the stage and let go of their hands long enough to raise one of his and snap his fingers.

In a minute a table was brought for us. Then Joe put a white towel over his arm and became our waiter. My children ordered hamburgers and fries and chocolate milkshakes. Joe bowed and said he would be right back.

I don't know that this is what happened next, but I can guess accurately. Joe would have gone behind the bar or into the kitchen and said to someone "Two burgers and fries and two chocolate milkshakes."

And then some want-to-be tough guy would have looked at him in horror. "We don't have chocolate shakes."

I know Joe would have looked at him and said, "I said two chocolate shakes." And then the tough guy would have had to run up and down Seymour Street in a panic with his eyes wide and his heart pounding looking for the only legal drink that the Penthouse ever sold.

He would have run south, then north, then circled and called his friends. "Where do you get a chocolate milkshake? I've got to get chocolate milkshakes or I'll be killed."

He probably went to White Spot, which had a habit of saving Saturday night dates with chocolate shakes, and came back with sweat running down his back (but not into the shakes) and handed them to Joe.

Joe put them on a serving platter along with the burgers and fries and carried them to our table.

"Enjoy," he said.

Joe was killed six years later, in 1983, during a robbery in the room where we drank coffee.

Now, almost thirty years after the robbery, I was looking at a painting of the Penthouse that was hung on the side of an old van. I tried to look through the same window behind which Joe and I drank coffee.

"Please, tell me more about yourself," I said to Keith.

Before he could answer, an old fellow with long white hair and a cowboy hat came along. He was Japanese in his ancestry, western in his headgear, and hard-working in the shopping cart filled with bottles that he was pulling.

"Hi, how you doing?" he said to Keith.

"You know him," I said, again being the master of the obvious.

"Sure, he's a good guy. I just wish he would put me in one of his pictures someday."

Keith called him Joe and they talked for a moment and then I asked Keith if he would ever include him in a painting.

"He's already there," said Keith.

Now here I was, about to meet a master of public relations. A long time ago I worked for a small-town newspaper in a small southern US town. The managing editor, who was also the only editor and, besides me, the only reporter, said there was one trick to selling papers: Put everyone's name in print at least once a year.

"Here," Keith showed Joe, "here you are."

I looked over Joe's shoulder and saw Keith pointing to a man with white hair and a cowboy hat in the corner of one of his paintings. All the many types of people who live here are in his paintings. That makes them authentic. The people inside their clothing may change, but their types do not. You can see clones in fitted suits on Howe or Robson Streets, just as you can see those who dress and act and move the same anywhere.

The story on television ended with Keith wrapping his Laughing Hand around Joe in a hug and Joe grinning from one side of his beard to the other. We showed the paintings. We showed his van. We showed him working.

The only thing that never made it into the story was the rusty fishing ball.

55

Eagles in the Sky

I just stopped writing and stepped outside. There were two eagles flying high overhead. They were incredibly beautiful.

They were not being harassed by crows, possibly because they were flying in air that was too high for their almost constant pains in the neck.

Crows drive eagles out of their minds, or at least I think they do. Every time I see eagles in the city they are surrounded by a gang of squawking black birds diving on them and trying to make life miserable.

I can't really blame the crows, because eagles eat crows, especially crow babies.

They also eat seagulls, so seagulls attack eagles when they fly low enough.

On the other hand, we all have to eat, and most birdwatchers would vote in favour of eagles over crows and seagulls.

I have done numerous stories on eagles and that's because a quarter century ago they were rare. None were nesting in Vancouver.

That was partly because I killed them.

I didn't mean to. I didn't know I was doing it, and I apologize, but I was part of the reason they almost disappeared.

This is another story that you may know, but from my personal survey, you probably don't.

When I was in the US Air Force, the first duty I had was with a civil engineering squadron in charge of killing any natural invader on the air base.

This included mosquitoes, which gummed up the intakes on the supersonic jets and stung the colonels and generals when they played golf.

To do this I spread DDT over the base. Every morning at 6 a.m. I rode in the back of an Air Force pickup truck with a large, powerful blower and 500 pounds of DDT.

I would pour the cardboard barrels of the poison into the top of the blower, start the engine on it, and wait for the truck to move. Then I would open the mouth of the blower and out would come a cloud of white dust, so thick it covered everything and made everything disappear.

I would pull on the handle that held the mouth open until the sergeant who was driving would stop and then I would load up the blower again and we would take off. We drove past the hospital, around the barracks and along the flight line, and most important of all, we rode over the golf course.

Everywhere we went the air was thick with a white trail of DDT. I was covered with it. But I was told, as a low-ranking airman, "Don't worry. It won't hurt you. It only kills mosquitoes."

I had no face mask. I had no gloves. I was white from my Air Force cap to my Air Force boots. The powder coated my skin under my uniform. When I took off my shirt and my pants I was white.

When I sucked in breath through my nose it was white.

When I breathed through my mouth, which happened when we suddenly went around a corner, it was white.

"Don't worry. It only kills mosquitoes."

We drove over the ninth hole on the golf course.

Why does an air base built for killing need a golf course? That is a rhetorical question.

The truck went up in the air, mainly because the sergeant had pushed the accelerator to the floor having seen a hill.

The extremely heavy blower, which was not anchored to the truck, bounced up in the air. My foot slipped under it. The blower came down on my foot.

I yelled.

I pounded on the side of the truck.

The sergeant looked at me in the mirror and waved.

I yelled some more.

He gave me the thumbs up. We were winning the war.

Then he pulled over to ask why I was no longer blowing smoke.

"I'm pinned. I'm in pain. I can't move."

"Oh."

I had five broken toes in defence of the golf course.

After that I was briefly assigned to light duty, crawling under the barracks looking for termites that were crawling up the wooden supports and eating away at the foundation of the entire Air Force.

I learned one thing under those barracks. The military does things in a big way. Every half-inch floorboard was nailed onto a three-quarter-inch slab of plywood using three-inch nails. That left somewhere near a million two-and-a-quarter-inch daggers of wasted nails above my head while I was crawling below. Since then I have never liked the expression "heads up."

I was spreading that DDT in 1966, and it killed a lot more

than mosquitoes. It killed everything that came in contact with it. It also made the shells of eagles' eggs so thin that they broke under the warming weight of their mothers.

Eagles were disappearing. The American symbol of freedom was dying.

An incredible woman named Rachel Carson had written a book four years earlier. She was an environmentalist before environmentalists were born. She simply loved life and because of that don't ever think books are not among the most powerful things in history. She wrote a book she called *Silent Spring*, which said among other things that DDT was killing everything.

She was laughed at.

And more things died.

Then more people read her book and the laughter died down. It became assigned reading in schools and kids went home and told their parents that DDT was killing everything. Their parents said they learned from the army that DDT only killed mosquitoes.

In time, as always happens, parents started learning from their kids and they called their political representatives and said DDT is killing everything.

It took more time while the politicians stopped believing the military and eventually said, "We have just discovered that DDT is killing everything." That was 1972.

That was thirty-three years after it was first used.

By then there were almost no eagles left in America and few in Canada. It took a while, but the chemical gradually washed out of the veins of the earth and the shells of the eggs of eagles and other creatures started to harden.

And today I saw two eagles flying way up there. I said to them, "Hi. I'm glad we both made it."

56

Teddy Bear

He looked like a biker—there were tattoos up and down each arm—but I couldn't help looking through his windshield and saying, "Wow. That is amazing."

He leaned out of his driver's window and said I should see it from inside.

I stepped off the curb and looked.

"Are you kidding?"

His entire dashboard was covered with things—tiny dolls, coins, plastic flowers, pens, tiny cars, and more dolls.

Where? How? Why?

He said he worked at a car detailing shop and he got all of this from the vacuum cleaner at the end of the day. Everything was headed to the dump if he didn't save it.

He washed them and started gluing them onto his dash. First a few dozen, then many dozens. Then, 800 pieces later, I said, "If I was working right now I would ask if you would like to be on television but, sadly, this is my day off."

"Any time," he said.

He told me his name was Buddy Bear. It sounded like a nickname.

He told me the name of the detailing shop, but I forgot it. I didn't have a notebook. Mainly I was thinking that it would make a good story, but on one level. You see way down there about your knees? That level.

That was because he was a car detailer. There wouldn't be much else in his life, I thought, because when you spend your life cleaning out cars there's not much time for social development.

In short, once again, I am narrow-minded and prejudiced and I understand everyone who forms opinions instantly, no matter how wrong we know that is.

A week later I am desperately trying to figure out what to do, because I have been at the dentist all morning having my teeth cleaned and I am dizzy from being upside down for more than an hour and I am still trying to remember the way I have been told to brush my teeth properly.

I swear I will be dying and some dental hygienist will be telling me I must go back and forth and then sweep up, or down, to get into all the nooks and crannies.

I have been brushing my teeth longer than the hygienist's parents have been alive. I still have teeth, some of them my own, and I am still being told how to do it.

And now I am desperate for something to put into the camera.

"Ahh, the detailer," I said to Dave McKay, the barbecue cameraman.

"Where does he work?" he asks.

There is a long silence on my part. Dave pulls over and starts looking up detailing places on his BlackBerry. This is impressive, because he's a country singer and a pulled-pork cooker. He is not a nerd.

I am a reporter and don't have a BlackBerry. I rely on the old-fashioned method. Prayer.

He finds a place that might be it. We go. It *is* it.

I remember the fellow's name is Buddy, but Buddy isn't there.

"I'll call Buddy Bear and get him here," says the owner.

That would be nice, I think, but I don't want to disturb him on his day off.

"He is never off," says the owner.

That is dedication. In ten minutes a gleaming fifteen-year-old Lincoln swings into the parking lot, out steps Buddy and I am happy. He shows us his dashboard full of salvaged toys and I am happier. That is enough for a story. You would be satisfied with that, a man with 800 trinkets pulled from a vacuum and glued to his dashboard, right? I was.

Besides, he works in a detailing shop. What else could there be?

He sees me looking at his tattoos. I think he looks like a biker.

"Here is one you will never see on a biker," he says. He is reading my mind, or the mind of everyone who has very small minds.

He holds up his arm and points to three candles and three words; "Faith, hope and charity," he says.

"And this is a Jewish sign of peace," he adds. "And underneath it says be kind to all."

And he is. He says he volunteers to help others. That's all he does and all he wants to do, besides spiff up his car.

Then he showed us a tiny picture of an old man whom he spent years assisting. The picture was on his dashboard. He pulled a picture of Jesus out of a pocket in the driver's door and said he always travels with him.

"Are you a Born Again Christian?" I asked, afraid, because some Born Again Christians make me wish I hadn't been born.

"No, I follow the Jewish religion," he said. "I met some Jews who were very kind to me. You see I was born an orphan. I never knew my parents. The Jews took care of me. Jesus takes care of me, and I take care of others. The *North Shore News* did a story about me once saying I was an unsung hero."

Oh, my lord. I forgot about the things glued to his dashboard.

"Is your name really Buddy Bear?"

He took out his driver's licence. Buddy Theodore Bear. Buddy Bear. Teddy Bear.

He showed us another tattoo. It said Bashir's. It was written across his chest. That was the name of the detailing company he worked for.

"I got tired of people asking how it's spelled."

WHAT?! No one has their employer's name tattooed on their chest.

"He is a very loyal employee," said his boss.

Can you imagine how clean your car would be if he did the work? He stands behind the company.

Never, I said to myself, never underestimate anyone. Never, do you hear me?

Never think that someone who cleans cars for a living has nothing else to tell you. Never think that someone who has armloads of tattoos doesn't wrap those arms around someone else who needs hugging.

Never prejudge anyone. Ever.

I think I am getting the lesson. Finally.

Thank you, Teddy Bear.

Last Chapter and Your Assignment

You remember that much earlier, back in Chapter 16, I said you and I could have a race to see who would first find enough stories to fill a book?

Well, you win, because I believe that since then you have looked for something odd and wonderful and you have found it. You found it in your children's eyes and in the smile of the old lady to whom you said hello at the bus stop, and you found it when you stopped to ask someone about those weird things on his dashboard.

When you begin doing that, it's amazing how many things you find—every flower and every funny-looking dog being walked by a funny-looking person. And you don't say, "That's a funny-looking dog." You say, "What a beautiful dog," and they will tell you they got the dog because it was unwanted because it was so ugly, but they thought it was beautiful. And you just told them the same thing.

Most of my stories take longer to tell because I haven't learned to make them brief, like your stories.

Start recording those stories. Just take notes at first, and then put them together. Skip television. Sit at a computer or get a pad and a ballpoint pen and write them down. When you get a swack of them, send them to a publisher.

Rejection. Rejection. And, oh, you might as well give up.

And then in the mail, "Yes, we would be interested in looking at some more of your stories."

Alternatively, don't worry about sending them to anyone. Just tell them to everyone.

And then write to me and we will start the race over again. And you will win, because you will be fresh and new at it and the world will open up.

It will be the thing that changes your life, or the life of someone you tell your stories to. You will spread good news. You will make the world a better place.

Just find it, record it in your beautiful mind, and tell it. You can also doctor it up so that it's complimentary to the person you are talking about. You can add excitement just in the way you are telling it. You can get sympathy or laughter.

You can create your own world, even for just a moment.

Remember the first line of the Bible? In the beginning God created the heavens and the earth.

That was a heck of a lot of creating.

You can create a story. And that will be just the beginning.

One final, final note.

Judy, Good Luck.